THE
CHRISTMAS
POCKET BIBLE

THE
CHRISTMAS
POCKET BIBLE

GUY & STEVE HOBBS

First edition published in Great Britain in 2009 by Crimson Publishing,
a division of Crimson Business Ltd.
This reprint first published in Great Britain in 2022 by Crimson
An imprint of Hodder & Stoughton
An Hachette UK company

1

Paperback ISBN 978 190708 700 4

Printed and bound in Great Britain by Clays Ltd, Elcograf S.p.A.

Hodder & Stoughton policy is to use papers that are natural, renewable
and recyclable products and made from wood grown in sustainable
forests. The logging and manufacturing processes are expected to
conform to the environmental regulations of the country of origin.

Hodder & Stoughton Ltd
Carmelite House
50 Victoria Embankment
London EC4Y 0DZ

www.hodder.co.uk

CONTENTS

ACKNOWLEDGEMENTS

The Hobbs brothers would like to thank their parents, Joan and Chris Hobbs, for many wonderful Christmases, past and future, and for making Christmas something worth writing about.

INTRODUCTION

Did you know an original 12th-century mince pie could weigh up to 100kg? And were you aware that kissing under the mistletoe derives from a Norse myth, thousands of years older than Christianity itself? Perhaps you have always wondered why we celebrate Christmas when we do? If so, *The Christmas Pocket Bible* is for you.

For many of us, Christmas is an annual holiday of over-consumption, family tension and frantic last-minute shopping that we have come to take for granted. In some 800 million family homes around the world, Christmas has become an annual celebration that crosses cultures and religions.

It is one of the oldest holidays mankind has and a multi-billion pound global industry has grown up around servicing our annual Christmas needs. Yet every year we go through the same routines and customs of overeating, dressing the tree and hanging out our stockings on Christmas Eve without ever wondering 'Why?'

Is it possible that somewhere along the line the true meanings behind our modern Christmas traditions have been lost in a flurry of wrapping paper and cracker hats?

This book is intended to redress that balance. Packed with facts, trivia, recipes and helpful advice, *The Christmas Pocket Bible* contains everything you need to know to become a Christmas expert.

From making your own Christmas pudding to throwing the perfect festive bash, we hope that in these pages you will find the answers to all your Christmas queries, plus a feast of helpful tips guaranteed to put the pop into your Yuletide popularity.

You will also find here the real stories that go to make up our modern Christmas traditions, from the ancient Roman feast of Saturnalia to the invention of our very own Santa Claus, while all the time never forgetting the birth of one Jesus Christ, of course.

Untangling the myths, legends and dogma that go to make up this most ancient of feasts, we have tried here to put Christmas into both a historical and traditional context, while at the same time remaining faithful to the true reason for the season.

We hope that the result is a useful and comprehensive reference guide to all things Christmas and that this book will become as much a part of your annual holidays as cold turkey sandwiches and mince pies. Merry Christmas one and all.

CHRISTMAS TRADITIONS

Many of the modern Christmas traditions that we take for granted have their origins far back in the mists of time.

❄ ADVENT CALENDARS ❄

Like many of our modern Christmas traditions, the advent calendar is German in origin. As early as the 16th century it was often family habit in much of German-speaking Europe to mark the days of advent either with the daily lighting of candles or the marking off of days with chalk.

While controversy surrounds the origin of the first printed advent calendar (front-runner to this claim lies with Neues Tagblatt Stuttgart, a Stuttgart newspaper that included a free giveaway calendar in 1904), it is certain that by 1908 Gerhard Lang at Reichhold and Lang's printing office was creating mass-produced advent calendars in a variety of designs that lasted until the company went out of business in the 1930s.

As other calendars came onto the market, competition started to hot up over the treats that lay behind the calendar doors. In the run-up to the Second World War, religious images were soon supplemented with bible readings and passages and finally sweets, until wartime paper rationing led to the halt of calendar production.

Richard Sellmer in Stuttgart revived the tradition in 1946. By the end of the 1950s advent calendars had become popular throughout Europe and as soon as rationing ended in the UK chocolates started to appear behind the calendar's miniature doors. See p. 87 for how to make your own advent calendar.

Pocket fact ☆

For Christmas 2007, German nanotech scientists created the world's smallest advent calendar at the University of Regensburg. Etched onto a sliver of gallium arsenide and measuring 8.4 μm by 12.4 μm (micrometers or microns) it would take more than five million of these calendars to cover one postage stamp.

❄ CANDLES ❄

Burning candles during the winter festivities predates Christianity by thousands of years. Much like the Yule log (see p. 36) the light of the candle helped to keep evil spirits away from the house and helped to renew the sun's power around the time of the shortest day.

The candle was absorbed into the Christmas tradition and remained popular throughout history. In the 16th century the Protestant reformer, Martin Luther, famously compared the candle-lit tree to the starry heaven from which Christ descended.

During the Victorian era, it was traditional to light a candle on the first Sunday of advent, two candles on the second Sunday and so on, until all four were lit on the fourth Sunday. This custom has largely been replaced with a single candle that burns for an hour on each day of advent.

Christingle

A rather new Christmas candle tradition is celebrated in churches and schools during advent. The word Christingle means 'Christ light', and the first Christingle service took place in Germany on Christmas Eve 1747. The bishop wanted to find an easy way to teach people the true meaning of Christmas with a simple symbol, made from an orange and candle (see p. 123). The custom reached the Church of England over 200 years later in 1968 and services usually focus on children.

❊ CHRISTMAS CARDS ❊

The Christmas card is attributed to the Victorian patron of the arts, Sir Henry Cole. During a career that included managing the construction of the Albert Hall, organising the Great Exhibition of 1851, establishing London's Victoria and Albert Museum and introducing the penny post in 1840, few of Cole's achievements have had the global impact of the common Christmas card.

Pocket fact ☆

If the nine billion Christmas cards purchased in the UK and US in 2008 were laid end to end, they would circle the earth 54 times.

A busy, modern man, with a personal mission to 'beautify life', Sir Henry Cole commissioned prominent British illustrator John Calcott Horsley to create an original card that he could send out to family and business associates. While Horsley's design, featuring a family surrounded by plentiful food and wine, created uproar from the Temperance Society of the day, the cards themselves were a hit and quickly came to replace the more traditional and time-consuming Christmas letter.

These cards also proved themselves a pretty canny business idea and, capitalising on the popularity of his new penny post, Cole sold them at his Bond Street art gallery. Of the original 1,000 print run, 12 cards remain today in private collections, and in 2001 one of Cole's personally signed cards sold at auction for an incredible £22,250.

❄ CHRISTMAS CAROLLING ❄

The tradition of carol singing is actually older than Christmas itself. Originally part of Pagan ritual to celebrate the winter solstice (22 December), these songs were probably more associated with dance than singing and the word carol is most likely derived from the old French term, *carole* (from the Latin *choraula*), meaning dance of praise and joy.

By AD129 the first official Christmas carol was added to the early Christian canon, when Telesphorous, Bishop of Rome, had decreed that 'In the Holy Night of the Nativity of our Lord and Saviour, all shall solemnly sing the Angel's Hymn'.

As the new Christian Church spread across Europe new and old traditions became intermingled as Christmas came to be accepted by the hoi polloi. One such example of this lies in the ancient English tradition of wassailing – see box below.

By the Middle Ages, however, the Christian Church's reaction against the old customs meant that non-Latin Christmas songs had practically died out in Europe until 1223 when St Francis of Assisi reintroduced the practice of singing popular songs (See p. 123.)

Here we come a-wassailing

Wassailing is still a popular festive pastime in some areas of Britain but it has a history that stretches back long before the birth of Christ. Wassail was a hot alcoholic drink, a bit like mulled cider, that was used to toast the sun as it rose after the shortest day of the winter solstice in order to encourage a bountiful harvest. The tradition continued throughout early history and was gradually absorbed into the Christmas proceedings.

By the 16th century, drunken wassailing peasants had become quite a problem. They would stumble from house to house, singing carols and demanding gifts. Their belligerent attitude is evident in the wassailers' chant, 'We wish you a Merry Christmas'. After demanding figgy pudding they make it clear that 'We won't go until we get some'. The booze-fuelled peasants could often turn quite nasty.

Banned by the Puritans, the tradition fell from favour until it was enthusiastically revived by the Victorians, who turned it into the more genteel practice of carolling from door to door.

Aided by the emergence of professional travelling minstrels and then Johannes Gutenberg's printing press in Germany around 1439, the 15th century saw the appearance of the first versions of many of today's most popular carols.

After the Reformation (1517) and the rise of Protestantism across many European countries, the popularity of carolling took another dip, reaching its nadir in England in 1647 when Oliver Cromwell made popular celebrations of Christmas and other saints days illegal (see p. 130).

Carols at King's

For millions of people around the world Christmas officially begins with the Festival of Nine Lessons and Carols from King's College, Cambridge. First held on Christmas Eve, 1918, the service derives from an Order created by EW Benson (later Archbishop of Canterbury) for an 1880 Christmas Eve service held in a wooden shed outside Benson's home in Truro.

Introduced to the college by then Dean of King's, and ex-Western Front army chaplain, Eric Milner-White, the order of service has remained largely unchanged since 1919 and although successive organists have introduced new carols over the years, the service always begins with Once in Royal David's City. *The first verse of this carol is always sung, unaccompanied, by a lone choirboy. To this day, tradition dictates that none of the waiting choirboys knows which of them will sing the solo until just before the service begins.*

First broadcast by the BBC in 1928, the service has gone on uninterrupted (with the exception of 1930) for over 80 years, even continuing through the Second World War when the location of the service remained an open secret. Today, this delightfully British Christmas event is listened to by millions worldwide.

But you can't keep a good song down and by the 19th century carolling had firmly re-established itself in the new concept of the family Christmas, as popularised by contemporary literature including Charles Dickens' *A Christmas Carol* in which Scrooge threatens a caroller who comes to his door to sing *God Rest Ye Merry Gentlemen*.

❄ CHRISTMAS CRACKERS ❄

The man to blame for the obligatory paper hat-wearing and the abysmal jokes associated with Christmas dinner is the inventor of the cracker, Mr Tom Smith from east London. Another Victorian innovation, the cracker first made an appearance in 1847.

Smith, originally a confectioner, was inspired by the tissue-paper wrapped bon-bons he spied on a trip to Paris. With a twist at either end, they looked much like a miniature version of the cracker we know today. Smith imported these sugared almonds and found that the vast majority were bought at Christmas by young men as a gift for their sweethearts. So, the great entrepreneur came up with the idea of adding mottoes and simple love poems to his sweets.

These were competitive times and other manufacturers were quick to copy Smith's ideas. To stay ahead of the game, Smith added the crack mechanism by chemically impregnating paper strips, and a few years later he discarded the sweet, replacing it with a surprise gift. The modern day cracker was a hit and by the turn of the century, Smith's firm was producing more than 13 million a year.

When Smith died, his two sons Tom and Walter took over the business and it continued to flourish. Tom junior came up with the addition of the paper hat. By the end of the 1930s the love poems had evolved into jokes and limericks. The company is still flourishing today, making millions of crackers each year and exclusively creating crackers for the royal family. Over the years the firm has created special crackers to honour the suffragettes, war heroes and the Coronation, among others. Their largest ever cracker was nine metres (30ft) high.

Pocket fact ☆

During the Second World War, the Tom Smith Company was commissioned to create a device made up of bundles of cracker snaps. When a special string was pulled these devices mimicked the sound of machine gun fire and were used by soldiers in training.

❄ CHRISTMAS DECORATIONS ❄

Since long before the birth of Christ, evergreens have been used to decorate houses during winter festivals. Our Norse ancestors decorated their homes with fir branches, mistletoe, holly and ivy to remind themselves that light and life would return to the world once more (see box below).

But it wasn't until the Victorian era that manmade decorations took off. After Prince Albert introduced the Christmas tree to the homes of the masses (see p. 32), demand increased for items with which to adorn it. Before the invention of fairy lights, candles were extremely popular. This is a surprise given that they were mostly made of animal fat and so stank to high heaven, filled the house with smoke and presented a potential fire hazard.

Many early tree decorations were of the edible variety, with sweets and fruits being particularly popular. As time wore on, small presents and ornaments were also added to trees, and by the 1880s glass ornaments were the height of fashion.

Why is it bad luck to leave your decorations up after Twelfth Night?

Early pagan druids believed that evergreens (brought into the home at this time of year) could only possibly stay alive during the winter because they held magical properties. In fact they were believed to contain mischievous wood spirits who were only prevented from causing chaos during the 12 days of the winter solstice festival. Thereafter, they were free to run riot.

Astoundingly we have not managed to shake this superstition off in thousands of years of history, and although very few people know the reason why, it is still commonly held that leaving your decorations up too long will bring bad luck upon the household.

Baubles were created to replace the more traditional apples that were once hung on the tree (as a reminder of the forbidden fruit of the Garden of Eden). The tinsel and various dangly decorations that came later as commercialism crept into the festival have no real significance. But they look very nice.

❄ CHRISTMAS PRESENTS ❄

Gift giving at Christmas is as old as the story itself. After all, it's in the nativity story: three Kings bearing gold, frankincense and myrrh. In fact, the ancient Romans had been exchanging gifts at this time of year for hundreds of years before Caspar, Melchior and Balthasar drew up their first list. During the Roman festival of Saturnalia (17 Dec–25 Dec), a time of misrule would be in force when slaves became masters and enemies sent gifts. Amongst family and friends lucky fruit called stenae would also be exchanged. It goes without saying that feasting and excess played a large part in the proceedings.

By the time St Nicholas stepped into the Christmas picture, from modern day Turkey, around AD270 (see p. 11), the exchange of good luck offerings for a new year ahead was familiar throughout Europe. By the 16th century Christmas gift-giving had become a common part of the Christian festival in Britain and the Tudors took the annual gift giving so seriously they preserved their annual exchanges with the gentry in a dedicated Gift Role.

Pocket fact ☆

In 1580 Sir Philip Sydney enraged Queen Elizabeth I by trying to dissuade her from marrying the Duke of Anjou. In 1581 he made her a Christmas gift of a jewel-studded whip to show he was back in line.

This period also saw the Reformation create a new, protestant Christmas giver in the form of Christkind, put out to challenge St Nicholas' popularity on Christ's birthday. Usually depicted as a young girl with wings and a gold crown or hair, Christkind delivered presents on Christmas Eve and became accepted widely across German-speaking Europe.

The modern commercial Christmas did not really take off, however, until the late 19th century. In fact it took until 1888 for the first Santa's grotto to appear at a JP Roberts department store in Stratford. By 1889, though, he was everywhere and Christmas became all about the kids overnight.

The gift of giving

- *Christmas spending in the UK on gifts annually exceeds £8bn*
- *Around £78m worth of unwanted gifts are returned to shops each January*
- *41% of toys given as presents are broken by March*
- *The average gift costs about £25*
- *The average UK child gets their first Christmas stocking aged two*
- *They get their last aged 15*
- *36% of Brits now do all of their Christmas gift shopping online*
- *The phrase 'It's better to give than to receive' derives from the bible, Acts 20:35, and is attributed by Paul to Jesus: 'It is more blessed to give than to receive.'*

❊ CHRISTMAS STOCKINGS ❊

The link between footwear and gift giving may seem oblique, but it is one that has echoes in many cultural tales and countries around the world. Perhaps the first popular depiction of the Christmas stocking tradition appeared in America in 1863 when German-American illustrator Thomas Nast published his cartoon Christmas Morning showing children rummaging through stockings for gifts. Clement Clark Moore's famous seasonal poem, 'Twas the night before Christmas (see p. 19), first published in 1823, also contains two references to the stocking.

The original story of the Christmas stocking is attributed to the Greek Orthodox bishop, St Nicholas (also known as Nicholas of Myra), born in modern day Turkey around AD270. Among other things, St Nicholas is the patron saint of sailors, prostitutes, repentant thieves and pawnbrokers, but is still best known as one of the archetypes of our modern Father Christmas (see p. 17).

Among the many tales of charity and good works assigned to St Nicholas, legend has it that the saint got wind of the plight of a poor man with three daughters for whom he could not provide a dowry. In order to help this man without causing the embarrassment of offering him public charity, St Nicholas made a journey to the poor man's home during the night and tossed a bag of gold through the window to pay for the marriage of the eldest daughter. The second daughter's dowry was provided in a similar way, but when it came to the youngest it was winter and the window was firmly shut. So Nicholas quietly climbed on the roof and dropped the bag of gold down the chimney. It landed in a stocking that was hung by the fire to dry (or in a shoe in some accounts). Today the oranges left in stockings are said to represent these bags of gold.

Christmas footwear around the world
- *In China Muslin stockings are traditionally hung to be filled with gifts from Dun Che Lao Ren*
- *Le Père Noël fills children's shoes with gifts in France*
- *Italian children leave their shoes out on the night before Epiphany (5 Jan) to be filled by the good witch, La Befana*
- *In Holland, Dutch children traditionally fill their clogs with hay and carrots on Christmas Eve for Santa's reindeer*

❊ THE QUEEN'S SPEECH ❊

One of the more modern Christmas traditions is the reigning monarch's Christmas message to the Commonwealth. The very first message came from Queen Elizabeth II's grandfather, King George V, in 1932. It was broadcast on BBC Radio in the year that the Beeb received its royal charter.

Pocket fact ☆
The very first Christmas message, transmitted from Sandringham, began with the words, 'I speak now from my home and from my heart to you all.' But these weren't George V's own words. They were written for him by none other than the author Rudyard Kipling.

But it wasn't long before the tradition came under threat. Stammering George VI, who came to the throne in 1936, was unwilling to continue with the broadcasts and for three years the country muddled through without direction from its monarch. Fortunately, George was persuaded to boost the war effort with a

Christmas speech in 1939 and he continued the tradition until the year of his death.

Queen Elizabeth II's first message to the Commonwealth was broadcast on Christmas Day, 1952. The Queen has reigned over a period of innovation, breaking into television from 1957, and in 2006 the Queen's Christmas message was available to download as a podcast for the first time.

Pocket fact ☆

The traditional 3pm slot allows the speech to be broadcast simultaneously in 17 commonwealth countries around the world.

The Queen's most famous speech was transmitted on Christmas Day 1992. She expressed her sorrow at the *'annus horribilis'* which had seen the break-up of two family marriages, one divorce and a disastrous fire at Windsor Castle.

The 'alternative' Christmas message

Broadcast on Channel 4 every year since 1993, the alternative Christmas message comes from a contemporary and often controversial figure and is broadcast at the same time as the Queen's speech. So far the message has come from:

- *1993 – Quentin Crisp (author and gay icon)*
- *1994 – Revd Jesse Jackson*
- *1995 – Brigitte Bardot*
- *1996 – Rory Bremner (as Princess Diana)*
- *1997 – Margaret Gibney (a Belfast schoolgirl, speaking on peace in Northern Ireland)*

- *1998 – Neville and Doreen Lawrence (parents of race-killing victim Stephen Lawrence)*
- *1999 – Ali G*
- *2000 – Helen Jeffries (mother of CJD victim Zoe Jeffries)*
- *2001 – Genelle Guzman (9/11 survivor)*
- *2002 – Sharon Osbourne*
- *2003 – Barry and Michelle Seabourn (from the reality show,* Wife Swap*)*
- *2004 – Marge Simpson*
- *2005 – Jamie Oliver*
- *2006 – Khadijah (a veiled Muslim woman)*
- *2007 – Sgt Major Andrew Stockton (Afghanistan war veteran)*
- *2008 – President of Iran, Mahmoud Ahmadinejad*

❈ PANTOMIME ❈

Like many festive traditions, the modern pantomime is a mixture of several historical customs and ideas:

- **The ancient Greeks.** The word pantomime comes from two Greek words: *panto* meaning 'all', and *mimos* meaning 'mimic'. Greek pantomimes starred a versatile solo performer who took on all the parts, accompanied only by a flute. Although quite different from the modern pantomime, the flexible nature of traditional gender roles and the key theme of a reversal of fortunes are recognisable.

- **Mystery and miracle plays.** One of the most popular forms of Christian entertainment, these plays were designed to help the illiterate learn the teachings of the bible. Stories from the Old Testament were performed around Christmas time and in the lead-up to Easter.

- **Mummers.** The medieval midwinter entertainment of mumming has its roots in a pre-Christian fertility rite. By the Middle Ages it had evolved into a form of village entertainment popular throughout the country, and even became part of the Christmas celebrations at court. The mummers wore elaborate masks, often in the form of animal heads. This tradition has survived in modern panto, where the traditional pantomime horse and Daisy the cow are staples. Father Christmas made an appearance in the mummers' plays, as did a cross-dressing Old Dame.

Cross-dressing in panto

During both the Roman festival of Saturnalia and the old English festival of Twelfth Night it was customary for the natural order of things to be turned on their head, so cross-dressing was quite normal (hence cross-dressing is a key theme in Shakespeare's Twelfth Night*).*

Many argue that these traditions fed into panto and explain why the pantomime dame is always played by a man, and the leading man often played by a woman. The clown Grimaldi is often credited with being the first official pantomime dame for his portrayal of Dame Cecily Suet in Harlequin Whittington in the 19th century.

- *Commedia dell'arte.* This Italian form of entertainment spread to British courts in the 16th century and was soon subsumed into the courtly Christmas masques of the time. The standard characters included lovers, a father and servants (one sly and the other a fool). This format makes up the basis of modern pantomime and during the 18th and 19th centuries traditional plots became mixed up with fairy tales and folk legends. Many of today's pantomime titles appeared at this time, including *Babes in the Wood, Aladdin* and *Cinderella*.

Pocket fact ☆

The 'father' of pantomime is a man called John Rich who founded the Covent Garden Theatre. His 18th-century ballet-pantomimes were extremely successful and were copied in other venues such as Sadler's Wells and the Theatre Royal in Drury Lane. These days, panto rarely makes an appearance in the West End, largely because foreign tourists struggle to get to grips with this uniquely British Christmas entertainment.

❋ FATHER CHRISTMAS ❋

SANTA: THE EARLY DAYS

Like so many Christmas traditions, the modern day Father Christmas is an amalgamation of customs, myths, legends, pagan beliefs, Christian beliefs and Victorian ideals.

The current image of Father Christmas didn't develop until well into the 19th century, but looking back in history there are a number of precursors to the great gift-giver, all of whom helped to give him the distinctive image and personality that we know so well today. Here are some of the best known:

- **Odin, chief of the Norse gods.** Some depictions of Odin are strikingly similar to how we imagine Father Christmas today. More than 6,000 years ago, Odin – with his long white beard, cloak and hat – would ride through the skies on an eight-legged horse. Known as the Old Man of Winter, he is shown in Scandinavian mythology bringing the snow and driving the reindeer herds on their migration. He was often accompanied by a Dark Helper – a horned demon who punished bad deeds, in contrast to Odin who rewarded the good with gifts. In many countries the Dark Helper is still a part of the Santa tradition (see p. 19).

- **Thor, the Norse god of thunder.** Another Norse god that can be thrown into the mix is Thor, mainly because he rode across the sky in a chariot pulled by two enormous goats called Cracker and Gnasher.

- **Saint Nicholas.** A highly venerated Greek Orthodox bishop who lived in Turkey in the fourth century is probably the most important role model for the modern day Father Christmas. A wealthy man by inheritance, he devoted himself to the church and gave his riches away to those more needy than he (see below).

- **Old Father Christmas.** An older version of Father Christmas, also known as Yule, had developed in Britain by the 17th century, before being suppressed by the Puritans. This Father Christmas was accompanied by a Dark Helper, as Odin had been before him, who would punish naughty children, but he did not bring presents to children. In fact he had more in common with the pagan Lord of Misrule who was appointed to organise festivities such as dancing and feasting during the winter solstice. He was a sort of embodiment of Christmas that oversaw the seasonal community celebrations and people really weren't sure what he looked like. Early depictions of Father Christmas showed him as tall, short, thin, fat, a troll, an elf and a pagan druid.

The Legend of St Nicholas

The devout Nicholas is credited with having performed a number of miracles. He probably became patron saint of children because of the story in which he brought two murdered boys back to life by the power of prayer. But it was his charity that helped spread the cult of Nicholas after his death. The best-known example of this charity is the one that led to children hanging up stockings on Christmas Eve (see p.11).

> *Nicholas died on 6 December (some time in the fourth century), the date that the Catholic Church later designated St Nicholas' Day. In much of Europe, the legend of St Nicholas became mixed in with older pagan traditions until it was commonly held that he was the bearer of winter gifts. In early depictions, St Nicholas is shown with a long white beard, travelling through the skies on a horse. The legend of his tossing a bag of gold down the chimney to help a poor nobleman evolved into the more familiar notion that Nicholas would come down the chimney to leave gifts for those children who knew their prayers.*
>
> *In many countries 6 December is still the day that St Nicholas traditionally brings presents for the children, leaving them in stockings or a shoe.*

FATHER CHRISTMAS AS WE KNOW HIM TODAY

It wasn't until the Victorian era that the modern image of Father Christmas began to take shape in Britain, and when it did it came from the unlikeliest of sources – America. The older Father Christmas character in Britain had been suppressed by the Puritans and, along with many of the Christmas traditions, had never really recovered. But across the pond in the New World, a new figure based on European traditions was taking shape.

Dutch emigrants had brought the tradition of St Nicholas (or Sinter Claes, as they called him) with them to east-coast America. Somewhere along the way, the tradition moved from 6 December to Christmas Eve and the name Sinter Claes became anglicised by the English-speaking inhabitants of New York. By the early 19th century many American children expected Santa Claus to bring them presents on Christmas Eve.

But it was a poem by Episcopalian minister Clement Clarke Moore that really helped to cement this new figure as a key part of Christmas and added some crucial elements into the mix. *An account of a visit from Saint Nicholas*, written in 1822 and better known as *The Night Before Christmas,* described a jolly man with a round belly, dressed all in fur, and coming down the chimney. All of these features were brand new but the poem was an immediate hit, and so gradually they became engrained in the popular consciousness.

Pocket fact ☆

Clement Clarke Moore had studied the folklore of northern European immigrants, which may help to explain why his description of St Nicholas was more reminiscent of Germany's Dark Helper character – Pelz Nickel or fur-clad Nick. Before his poem, St Nicholas was usually depicted as a tall, thin, sombre man in ecclesiastical dress.

This new image was reinforced by illustrations drawn by American caricaturist Thomas Nast. His classic version of a portly, bearded Santa appeared in *Harper's Weekly* in 1863 and Nast continued to develop the image into the 1880s, by which time the character had gained the furry suit, hat, boots and wide belt.

It was during the 1860s that this new Santa figure crossed the Atlantic for the first time. He couldn't have arrived in Britain at a better time. The family-oriented Victorian Christmas was gaining momentum and the idea of giving gifts on Christmas Day rather than at New Year had just caught on. Although he kept the more traditional British name of Father Christmas, he eagerly took on all the new traits of his American counterpart.

BUT WHAT ABOUT THE REINDEER?

Moore's poem is also wholly responsible for the introduction of reindeer to the Santa legend. Before *The Night Before Christmas* the traditional mode of transport for St Nicholas was a flying horse, but Moore described 'a miniature sleigh and eight tiny reindeer'. He also named them:

Dasher
Dancer
Prancer
Vixen
Comet
Cupid
Donner
Blitzen

These are familiar names to us today, but in 1823 they had never been heard before.

Of course one key name is missing from Moore's poem. The most famous of all the reindeer, Rudolph, did not make an appearance until more than 100 years later. In fact it was Santa himself who had the red nose, 'like a cherry' in the poem.

Rudolph

Rudolph the Red-Nosed Reindeer *was a poem written by the copywriter Robert May in 1939. May worked for the Montgomery Ward chain of department stores in the USA and his poem was designed to attract customers. Ten years later, the composer Johnny Marks set the poem to music and it was released by Gene Autry, 'the Singing Cowboy'. The song has since been recorded by a whole host of artists and has sold more than 80 million copies worldwide.*

Pocket fact ☆

A single reindeer can pull double its own body weight for up to 40 miles. Impressive. But bear in mind that if Santa's sleigh contained just one toy for every child in the world, it would weigh over 400,000 tons. Santa would require more than a billion reindeer to pull his sleigh along the ground, let alone through the sky.

THE COCA-COLA CLAUS

The piece of Santa trivia you are most likely to hear in the pub involves the colour of his suit. It is commonly held that the Coca-Cola company is responsible for dressing Santa in its own corporate colours, and that prior to a 1930s advertising campaign by the drinks giant, Father Christmas wouldn't be seen dead in anything other than green.

This is certainly what Coca-Cola would have us believe, but how much truth is there in the claim? The old Father Christmas of British tradition was often clad in forest green, the stamp of the Lord of Misrule figure whence he came. However, early Christmas cards show that the red and white costume had started to become popular by the late Victorian era. But green was still common and some cards even show him in blue and purple.

Designed to encourage people to drink Coke in the winter, the advertisements designed by Swedish artist Haddon Sundblom first appeared in 1931. They featured a jolly Santa in a red tunic with white trim holding a glass of Coca-Cola rather than his trademark pipe. This campaign ran for over 30 years and was incredibly successful.

While Coke may not have invented the modern Santa image it seems likely that the longevity of this campaign and its international, commercial nature helped secure the dominance of one particular image over all the others that had gone before.

WHERE DOES SANTA LIVE?

In 1863 the illustrator Thomas Nast helped to create a custom that has become as much a part of Christmas for children as carols and mince pies. His illustration of that year showed Father Christmas reading a letter that had been sent to him by a child. From that moment on, in both Britain and America, children began writing to Santa to ask for specific presents.

Thus began another great Santa debate, still unresolved to this day. How should children address their letters? In Britain this issue was neatly sidestepped as it became common to either leave the letter by the fireside or put it up the chimney. Since Father Christmas came down the chimney it made sense that letters that disappeared up the chimney would eventually reach him, wherever he might be. In modern times of course, the chimney is quite a rarity and so a postal address has become all the more important.

Of course, St Nicholas originally came from Myra in modern day Turkey, but this has somehow never caught on as Santa's hometown. Icier regions have always been more appealing. It was a poem from 1869 by George Webster that first suggested the North Pole as Santa's home. Other suggestions that have entered popular myth include Greenland (from a 1933 Disney film, *Santa's Workshop*) and northern Finland (a myth started by a Finnish radio personality in the 1920s). The Lapland tourist board has since promoted the area around Rovaniemi in Finnish Lapland as Santa's home, developing a theme park and Santa's 'official post office', which handles 750,000 letters every year.

Sending your letter

The Royal Mail have made British children's lives a lot easier by circulating Santa's postal address. Enclose your letter and list, write clearly your name and address and attach either a first or second class stamp to the envelope.

Santa/Father Christmas
Santa's Grotto
Reindeerland
SAN TA1

Santa replies to everyone he can, although the Royal Mail do warn that it is a very busy time for him. To ensure you get a reply, write to him before 12 December.

Pocket fact ☆

In 1939, Orson Welles ran a spoof radio newscast in New York, announcing that Santa's workshop in the North Pole had been attacked by the Nazis. Without waiting to listen to the end of the seasonal allegory, thousands of children gathered at Macy's department store on 34th Street to weep for the death of Santa. New York mayor of the time, Fiorello LaGuardia, was only able to quell the disturbance by dressing up as Santa himself and appearing before them.

Traditional Christmas timings

Making the Christmas pudding. *Traditionally you should prepare the Christmas pudding on the last Sunday before advent, known as Stir-up Sunday.*

Making a Christmas cake. *This should be made at least a month in advance and should be fed once a week until Christmas Day. To feed the cake, poke holes in it with a skewer and pour over 1–2 teaspoons of brandy.*

Sending the cards. *Christmas cards can be sent any time during advent, but the best time to send them is about two weeks before Christmas. This should ensure that they arrive in plenty of time. If you're running late then check with Royal Mail for the last post dates. For international airmail it is best to leave 10–14 days.*

A Christingle service. *The symbolism of Christingle varies according to when it is held. If held during advent, then it represents the hope of light in the darkness. But if it is held on Christmas Eve, it symbolises the birth of Jesus.*

Decorating the house. *For the true traditionalist, Christmas Eve is the day to bring in the tree and put up the decorations. But most households do this the week before.*

Ordering presents online. *Order at least a week in advance, depending on where the weekend falls. Sites that are really geared up for Christmas, like Amazon, allow you to order as late as 23 December, or even Christmas Eve if you're prepared to pay through the nose.*

Taking the decorations down. *Bad luck will befall the household if the decorations are left up past Twelfth Night. Unfortunately there is some confusion over when Twelfth Night actually falls. According to the Church, it is Epiphany Eve, 5 January. This is because in centuries gone by Christmas was deemed to start at sunset on 24 December. However, nowadays most people count from Christmas Day and so Twelfth Night falls on the 6 January.*

❄ CHRISTMAS FOOD ❄

CHRISTMAS PUDDING

So good was his first taste of pudding that the Hanoverian King George I is said to have overturned a Cromwellian ban in 1714. It was around this time that the Christmas pudding evolved into the form we know today. George would almost certainly have been tucking into a huge suety ball, about the size of a football and set aflame with brandy. And it would have been deliciously, fermentedly sweet.

The pudding started out in the Middle Ages as a kind of spiced Christmas porridge which was eaten during the nativity fast which ran for the 40 days up to and including Christmas Eve, before excesses of feasting took place. It contained cracked wheat, meat broth or milk and maybe some currants and fruits. As Christmas Eve was a strict fast day until the first star was seen, gradually Christmas Eve frumenty got heavier and more indulgent, until finally it graduated to its rightful place at the Christmas Day feast.

Elizabethan recipes thickened the mix further with breadcrumbs and then suet, still adding meat and onions into the fruity stodge. By the end of the 17th century the meat had gone to be replaced with alcohol-marinated fruits and the practice began of making it months before and storing it.

Pocket fact ☆

In Tudor times the ingredients of Christmas pudding were wrapped in a pig's gut before being boiled (like a haggis). Over time, people started rolling the ingredients into a ball, wrapping it in hessian cloth, and then lowering it into boiling water. This is what gave the Christmas pudding its trademark cannonball shape.

The making of a Christmas pudding is steeped in ritual, tradition and superstition. Many say it should only be made on the last Sunday before advent, also widely considered to be the last day on which a Christmas pudding can be made to give it enough time to mature. This day is known as Stir-up Sunday, which is not for the reasons you might think, but because the prayer book for that day says 'Stir up, we beseech Thee, O Lord, the will of thy faithful people.'

(See p. 54 for the Pocket Bible traditional Christmas pudding recipe.)

Pudding-making superstitions

- *Ensure the pudding has been made before the 25th Sunday after Trinity Sunday (usually at the end of May or beginning of June)*
- *The pudding should contain 13 ingredients to honour Christ and his disciples*
- *Each member of the family should stir the mix*
- *The mix should be stirred from east to west, after the three wise men*
- *You can make a wish as you stir the mix*
- *Coins are sometimes put into the mix for luck and wealth for the year ahead*

CHRISTMAS CAKE

While the roots of the modern Christmas cake have become inexorably connected to that of plum pudding, the Christmas cake as we know it today derives from a drier cake traditionally served on Twelfth Night. King Cake, as it was also known, was traditionally eaten to celebrate the arrival of the Three Kings to Bethlehem at Epiphany.

King Cake has a rich tradition all of its own. Twelfth Night was through medieval times a period of raucous misrule, presided over by a mock king. Although many methods were used to select the king for the day, often a bean would be baked into the cake and the finder appointed Lord of Misrule.

As Twelfth Night started to be eclipsed by Christmas Day after 1860, the cake gradually migrated to its now familiar place, served with tea, late on Christmas afternoon.

(See p. 58 for the Pocket Bible Christmas cake recipe.)

MINCE PIES

The grand tradition of mince pie baking began in the 12th century when knights returning from the Holy Land introduced enticing new spices. Cinnamon, cloves and nutmeg, representing the gifts bestowed on Jesus by the Three Wise Men, were added to pies baked to celebrate Christ's birthday.

But Christmas pies, as they were originally known, were quite different from those that we enjoy today. Among the dried fruit and spices was an unfamiliar ingredient: shredded meat, including goose, veal, rabbit, pigeon and whatever was available at the time. This is where the 'mince' in the name comes from.

Pocket fact ☆

Whereas fruit and spices are the main constituent of today's mince pie, it is likely that they were only added to the pies of the Middle Ages to hide the flavour of rancid meat.

Not only were medieval mince pies quite different in flavour, they also looked very different. It was customary to make one large pie for the whole family to enjoy throughout the festive season, and as a result they were enormous. Weighing up to 100kg, they often had to be held together with metal clamps during the baking process.

By the Tudor period, these pies had become known as 'crib pies' because they were baked in the shape of the baby Jesus' crib. The more skilled pastry chefs of the era even created a little pastry baby Jesus to go on top.

But trouble was brewing for the enormous meaty Christmas pie. When Cromwell's government banned Christmas and all its trimmings in the 17th century (see p. 130), the pies were also outlawed. Thankfully, they didn't disappear, they were just forced underground. First to go was the obviously festive name and from then on they became known as minced or shredded pies. Secondly they lost their conspicuous shape and vast girth, becoming the small, round pies they are today. The mince pie was thus able to avoid detection and survive this terrible period of pie persecution.

Further changes took place over the years and by the end of the 19th century meat was no longer included, although the suet remained as a way to preserve the mixture.

Remember, folklore decrees that if you eat at least one mince pie on each of the Twelve Days of Christmas you can be certain of good fortune for the year ahead.

Pocket fact ☆

The expression 'to eat humble pie' actually refers to a 17th-century type of Christmas or mince pie eaten by the lower classes. Umble pie, a corruption of numble pie (from the French word nomble) was made of deer's innards and other offal, as well as the traditional fruit and spices.

CHRISTMAS DINNER

These days we expect to see turkey or goose on the Christmas table, but this wasn't always the case. During the early medieval Christmas feasts, the head of a wild boar was the prized component. Royalty and noblemen enjoyed hunting the beast (which was later hunted to extinction) and the head was served up with an orange or apple in its mouth, to a fanfare of trumpets and singing.

Other popular meats at medieval Christmas feasts were mutton and various forms of game, often served in a pie. By the Victorian era, especially in the north, roast beef had become the most popular red meat to be eaten at Christmas.

But birds have also been a longstanding feature of the Christmas menu including pheasant, pigeon, capon and swan. In the middle ages, the peacock was very popular, more for its appearance than taste. The bird was skinned rather than plucked and the roasted meat was sewn back into its skin before serving. Swan was another Christmas meat enjoyed by the upper echelons of society. The aristocracy felt that the bigger and more impressive the bird, the better, but it is the goose that is the most traditional of all the Christmas birds.

Goose

Even the rural poor could afford to keep a few geese. As well as providing the Christmas feast, the added benefit of geese was that they acted as an early burglar alarm, and their grease had useful medicinal properties.

In Victorian Britain, goose clubs were established as a sort of savings scheme for the poor. By saving a little each week, less wealthy citizens could guarantee themselves some goose to eat on Christmas Day. This is what the Cratchit family have done in

Dickens' *A Christmas Carol*, before Ebenezer Scrooge arrives with the best turkey in the shop.

> *Pocket fact* ☆
>
> *Queen Elizabeth I is said to have been enjoying roast goose at Greenwich Palace on Christmas Eve 1588, when she heard the news that the Spanish Armada had been destroyed.*

Turkey

It is odd that the turkey has become the staple British Christmas lunch, given that it is not native to Britain, or indeed Turkey. The turkey originally came from Central America and so didn't appear in Britain until the early 16th century.

It was early American settlers who introduced turkey as a festive treat, being far more common in the New World than the goose. The turkey was introduced to central Europe by Turkish traders and so became known as the turkey-cock. From the mid-16th century turkeys were reared in Norfolk, a bootiful tradition that the great Bernard Matthews keeps alive today.

> *Pocket fact* ☆
>
> *As the demand for a Christmas turkey grew in London and other urban areas, it became necessary for hundreds of turkeys to be marched to the capital from the breeding areas of Norfolk and Suffolk. Such was the distance that farmers had to create tiny leather or sack boots to counter the considerable wear and tear the poor birds suffered to their feet.*

Europeans were clearly very confused about the origins of this Central American bird. While the British called it the turkey, the

French, Italians and Germans all called it the Indian chicken (*coq d'Inde, galle d'India, indianische henn*), on account of Columbus mistakenly discovering America while looking for an alternative route to India.

Queen Victoria and Prince Albert were instrumental in popularising the turkey, as with so many Christmas traditions. They famously swapped their swan for turkey in the 1850s, and those who could afford it ditched their traditional goose in order to follow suit.

❄ CHRISTMAS FLORA AND FAUNA ❄

THE CHRISTMAS TREE

One of the earliest references to the Christmas tree appears in the Old Testament Book of Jeremiah, where the prophet condemns the ancient Middle Eastern custom of decorating trees as a heathen ritual, saying 'For the customs of the people are vain: for one cutteth a tree out of the forest, the work of the hands of the workman, with the axe. They deck it with silver and with gold; they fasten it with nails and with hammers, that it move not' (Jeremiah 10:2–4).

Fast forward around 1,000 years to the eighth century AD and we find another important Christian character, St Boniface, raging against tree worship, cutting down a German oak he found a group of pagans worshipping. According to this legend a fir tree sprang from the roots of the fallen oak, which Boniface took to represent the Christian faith.

As a result of this Germanic legend the decoration of fir trees at Christmas remained popular, particularly around the Rhine valley, and Martin Luther, the father of protestantism, is credited with decorating evergreen bowers with the help of his congregations throughout the 16th century in Germany. Records also show a Christmas tree erected at Strasbourg Cathedral in 1539 and by working men's guilds in Bremen and Basle by 1597. By the 17th century the custom had started to spread into family homes.

It was Queen Victoria who popularised the tradition in England after her marriage to German Prince Albert in 1843. Albert's annual family gift of a richly decorated fir tree outside Windsor Castle caught the imaginations of England's new moneyed class after a print appeared in the *Illustrated London News* of the royal family gathered around their tree in 1848, and the tradition quickly became a London fashion.

Pocket fact ☆

For Victorians, a good Christmas tree had to be six branches tall and placed on a table covered with a white damask tablecloth. It was decorated with wreaths, sweets and flowers.

Choosing the tree

- *Norway spruce — Traditionally Britain's favourite tree, it has lost favour in recent times for shedding needles. Keep well watered and away from radiators to lose fewer needles.*
- *Nordmann fir — Dark green needles with a silvery under-side, this is the original non-drop tree.*
- *Fraser fir — Smaller than the Nordmann fir, but with the same needle-holding ability, this is the tree for apartment dwellers.*
- *Blue spruce — A silvery-blue colour and thick needles with that citrus Christmas tree scent.*
- *Scots pine — Extra long needles make for a bushy tree that won't drop all over your carpet.*

HOLLY

In these days of mass consumption and Christmas commercialism, going green for the holiday period may sound like a modern idea but in fact it is the oldest of all our Christmas traditions. When it comes to everything evergreen we have the Nordic and Celtic pagans to thank for most of our traditional festive foliage.

In the earliest pagan traditions, winter solstice or Yule (21/22 December) was a time to celebrate the return of the sun god and evergreens were used to ward off evil spirits during the dark months of winter. Of these evergreens, holly was the most powerful.

Holly's powers

- Throughout the British Isles the Celts believed the Holly King ruled over winter and death.

- Holly was also associated with luck and fortune because its continued colour during the winter months reflected the eternal nature of mother earth.

- It was also the plant of immortality.

- In the Nordic pagan traditions holly also belonged to Thor, the god of thunder and lightning, and was believed to ward off lightning strikes, so was often planted near to very ancient settlements.

- Holly also played an important part in the celebrations of the Roman winter feast of Saturnalia, when Saturn, the god of harvest, was honoured in order to settle all accounts for the previous and coming year's harvest.

Boughs of holly would be used as decorations in homes and through the streets of Rome and it seems likely that early Christians adopted these holly decorations of the winter celebrations for their own

Christmas celebrations in order to blend in with the local pagan population and avoid persecution.

Today holly has become closely associated with Christian iconography, particularly Christ's crown of thorns on the cross (sometimes also said to be made from holly wood), with the plant's red berries said to come from the drops of His blood.

Pocket fact ☆
In medieval times, disputes were often settled under a holly tree. It was thought to speed negotiation and lend longevity to the outcome.

IVY

In many ways ivy was seen by early cultures to be the feminine ying to holly's more masculine yang. Like her more prickly brother, ivy was linked to immortality, protection from evil and rebirth. Ivy, however, was seen as the weaker, needing support in order to grow, but then offering support and protection in return. The intertwining of holly and ivy in wreaths symbolised the natural balance of the masculine and feminine in life and many have read the classic Christmas carol, *The Holly and the Ivy* to be a song about the battle between the sexes. It was probably sung to accompany a ritual mating dance and through the centuries there are recurring references to country dances between men carrying holly and women bearing ivy boughs.

For the ancient Romans ivy was strongly associated with Bacchus, the god of wine, and ivy was said to prevent intoxication and confer the power of prophecy. As Christian iconography began to absorb these ancient beliefs, ivy has come to be associated with the Virgin Mary, while holly represents Christ.

MISTLETOE

A favourite of the British druids, mistletoe was thought to be a cure for absolutely everything. Because the plant bears its fruit at around the time of the winter solstice (Yule), popular legend has it that mistletoe was gathered by druids at this time and had to be cut with a gold sickle and collected before it touched the ground or it would lose its power. There isn't a lot of evidence for much of this though. It was, however, certainly a revered plant used widely in ceremonies and, along with holly and ivy was used for protection against evil spirits.

Kissing under the mistletoe

In Norse myth, the goddess of love, Frigga, has a son named Balder. She loves him so much she makes all things on earth swear an oath not to harm him — except mistletoe (which slipped through on the technicality of being neither wood, water, earth nor air). Inevitably the god of evil, Loki, stumbles upon this loophole, fashions an arrow from mistletoe and, in a nice twist, gets Balder's blind brother to deliver the coup de grace. Happily, Frigga is able to revive Balder with the use of mistletoe and so she blesses the plant, promising a kiss to all who pass under it. Except Loki, presumably.

Secretly everyone's favourite Christmas tradition, kissing under the mistletoe, is a leftover from our Viking heritage and derives the Norse myth of Frigga and Balder (see below). Surviving the centuries in one form or another, it was the Victorians who really popularised the tradition, allowing as it did a level of flirting otherwise entirely frowned upon in public. There was a caveat. With each kiss, a berry had to be removed from the sprig and when the berries ran out, the kissing stopped.

THE YULE LOG

Coming particularly from Norway and Denmark, this ancient Scandinavian custom originally involved the burning of a huge log for the entire 12 days of Yule, the name given to the Viking winter feast. At the time of the winter solstice, the men would go into the woods and come back with the largest log they could find.

In the frozen north of Europe, the amount of daylight in the bleak midwinter is either minimal on non-existent. And in ancient times, this was a period of fear and superstition. The burning of the Yule log symbolised light and new birth at a time when the world was drenched in darkness and decay, and was a sign (along with evergreens that were brought into the house) that life could persist through the dark days.

The tradition probably came to Britain from Scandinavia via the Vikings, and was absorbed into Celtic folklore. Only by keeping the Yule log alight for those 12 days would the sun return and the days grow longer.

Pocket fact ☆
To the Celts, the Yule log represented prosperity for the years to come, but should the burning log go out within 12 days then bad fortune would fall upon the household.

By the Middle Ages, Christianity had supplanted pagan belief, but the Yule log remained and each year a huge piece of timber was hauled into the household with great ceremony and lit from a piece of the previous year's log. By the Victorian period it had become customary to keep the log burning only for 12 hours, rather than 12 days. And today the custom exists as nothing more than a table decoration, or a delicious chocolate confectionery, the recipe for which can be found on p. 60.

ROBINS

The humble robin redbreast, his ruddy plumage offset by the crisp white snow around him, is an enduring symbol of the festive season. Still active in winter, this friendly bird has long been an omen of good luck and in many parts of Britain it was customary to make a wish on the first sighting of the year. Oddly enough no one really knows why, of all the birds, it is the robin that appears on our Christmas cards. But of course, there are lots of theories and legends that attempt to explain the association:

- The most appealing of the explanations comes from a legend surrounding the nativity (see box below). Sadly it is unlikely that this story was well enough known to explain the popularity of the robin as a Christmas symbol.

- Another legend places the robin at the crucifixion. According to this story a plain brown bird removed a thorn that had dug into Jesus' head from the crown of thorns. As the snagged thorn came free it splashed Christ's blood onto the robin's breast, which remained as a symbol of the robin's Christian charity. Interesting though this story is, it is surely more relevant to Easter than Christmas.

- Some theories link the robin to Father Christmas. Early accounts of Father Christmas include a 'Dark Helper', who, from the 17th century, was often depicted as the figure known as Robin Goodfellow. It is possible that cards showing a robin perched on the shoulder of the jolly gift-giver may be the last remnants of an older Father Christmas story.

- In Victorian Britain, postmen who wore the red uniforms of the Royal Mail were nicknamed Robins. Some have argued that the robin came to represent not Christmas, but the bringer of Christmas goodwill, the postman himself.

How the robin got his red breast

In the days following the birth of Jesus, Joseph popped out for wood to feed the fire that was keeping the newborn warm. But he was quite some time and Mary feared that the fire would go out before he returned. At this point a flock of plain brown birds flew into the stable and made a circle around the fire, beating their wings to fan the flames and keep it alight. When Joseph returned and all was well again, Mary noticed that the birds had scorched their breasts in their heroic effort. She blessed the birds for their generosity and named them Robin Redbreast.

2

FOOD AND DRINK

The celebration of the birth of Christ has been associated with gastronomic excess and overindulgence for hundreds of years.

Unlike other religious observances where restraint, guilt and even abstinence are the order of the day, Christmas is a time that has long been associated with feasting. So when you're polishing off a box of Quality Street, or tucking into your fourth turkey sandwich, just remember that your medieval forebears would have been indulging in boar's head, peacock, and even swan.

So come on, eat a mince pie for each of the apostles, dig in to a second helping of figgy pudding, and leave the guilt until New Year, because tradition decrees it.

❄ CHRISTMAS LUNCH ❄

Cooking Christmas lunch can be a source of grave stress and last-minute panic. But as every Boy Scout knows, the trick is to be prepared. Leave yourself plenty of time, and plan the meal with the precision of a military operation, and you might just get out unscathed. The Pocket Bible Christmas Menu should also help.

TURKEY

In the UK, more than 10 million turkeys are routinely gobbled up on Christmas Day each year (see p. 30) and the leftovers enjoyed in sandwiches for days to come. This succulent recipe will provide enough for eight adults, with leftovers for four.

The Pocket Bible Christmas Menu
Christmas Lunch
Succulent roast turkey (or goose or nut roast)
Traditional sausage and apple stuffing
Pigs in blankets
Roast potatoes with rosemary
Honey-glazed parsnips
Leeks and Brussels sprouts with toasted almonds
Port and cranberry sauce
Luxury bread sauce
Special gravy

———

Traditional Christmas pudding
or
Rich almond, Guinness and whisky mince pies
served with brandy or rum butter

Christmas Afternoon Tea
Last-minute Christmas cake
or
Chocolate Yule log

NB – all recipes serve eight unless otherwise stated.

Pocket Recipe: Succulent roast turkey

3.6–4.5kg oven-ready turkey
sausage and apple stuffing (see p. 50)
25g–50g softened butter
fresh sage, bay and vine leaves, to garnish

1. Remove the giblets. Ideally this should be done on Christmas Eve and the giblets used to make a stock for the gravy (see p. 51).

2. Stuff the bird at the neck end, moulding the skin over the top to give the turkey a rounded shape.

3. Tuck the excess skin underneath the bird, and tie the turkey's legs together with ovenproof string.

4. Place the turkey in a roasting tin lined with a large piece of foil. Spread the butter over the turkey's skin and season. Bring the foil round and join at the top to enclose the turkey.

5. Roast at 190°C (gas mark 5) for 3½ to 4 hours, opening the foil for the last 40 minutes. Check that the juices run clear.

6. Cover with foil and leave to rest for half-an-hour. This will make carving much easier.

Don't forget: Christmas Eve

- *Remove the turkey giblets and use them to make stock for the gravy.*
- *Make the cranberry sauce and the bread sauce.*
- *Prepare the stuffing.*
- *Re-wrap the Christmas pudding if necessary.*
- *Calculate when to put the turkey in the oven, depending on when you want to serve lunch, and remember to add 30 minutes' resting time before carving.*
- *Make the mince pies, while listening to carols from King's (using pastry made beforehand and frozen).*

Pocket fact ☆

Even though turkey was long established as the Christmas lunch staple by Victorian times, Queen Victoria herself insisted on eating a seasonal swan right up to the 1850s. Don't follow her example, though, since all swans are protected by law (since 1981) and the mute swan has been owned by the Crown since as far back as 1482.

GOOSE

An alternative to Christmas turkey, and actually more traditional, is goose (see p. 29). In medieval England goose was the most popular Christmas bird, followed by chicken and capon. Even the rich who preferred gilded peacock, would often sew a roast goose inside the skin and feathers of the elegant bird. Peacock, it turns out, doesn't actually taste very nice.

Goose should be cooked in a moderately hot to hot oven (200°C–220°C or gas mark 6–7). Allow five minutes per 450g, plus 15 minutes.

Pocket tip △

Poorly prepared goose can be very fatty. To allow the fat to run away, follow these simple tips:

1. *Never cover a goose when roasting.*
2. *If possible, stand on a rack in the roasting tin so that the fat runs away into the tin.*
3. *After the bird has been cooking for 30–40 minutes, prick the skin lightly and the excess fat should come squirting out. Do this at 30-minute intervals during roasting. Be careful doing this: if you prick too deeply, the fat runs into the flesh rather than out of it.*

VEGETARIAN CHRISTMAS

There are many great seasonal flavours that don't involve meat, so it's easy to cater for vegetarians at Christmas. Remember to keep your veggie guests in mind when preparing the trimmings – you will need to make a separate meat-free gravy, for example, and you should keep the meat separate when serving. For better or worse, the classic vegetarian Christmas dinner is the nut roast:

Pocket Recipe: Luxury nut roast (serves 4)

250g mixed nuts (walnuts, hazelnuts, sesame seeds, almonds, cashew nuts)
400g tinned chopped tomatoes
100g shallots, finely chopped
1 egg, beaten
100g grated cheddar
½ tsp each of dried thyme, sage and mint
1 tbsp finely chopped parsley
1 tsp freshly squeezed lemon juice
1 tsp Marmite blended with 1 tsp boiling water

1. Toast the nuts in a dry frying pan over a moderate heat until golden. Leave to cool and then grind in a food processor. Preheat the oven to 180C (gas mark 4).

2. Combine the ground nuts in a mixing bowl with all of the other ingredients and mix thoroughly.

3. Scoop the mixture into a well-greased loaf tin and bake for around an hour until firm and golden. Allow to cool slightly before turning out and serving.

Catering for large numbers

Cooking huge quantities of food can be extremely stressful and difficult to time correctly. With a little planning you should be fine. These tips should help:

- *Check that the fridge and oven are large enough to store and cook all of the dishes you want to prepare. If the fridge is too small, use the garage or shed to store vegetables, puddings and pies, making sure all the food is well wrapped.*
- *Make sure that food to cook in the oven can be cooked at the same temperature.*
- *Make a time plan in advance and stick to it with military precision. That way things will get done efficiently and nothing will be forgotten. Allow extra time to do everything so you don't get in a panic.*
- *Do as much of the preparation as you can in advance. Chop up the vegetables, mix the stuffing, make the pastry and do anything else you can the day before.*
- *Although it may seem like cheating, there's no shame in using the microwave when you're catering for a large group.*
- *If you have more guests than table space, then make your menu more practical. A buffet meal may well be more appropriate, and you will be far less stressed if you keep it simple.*

VEGETABLES

Pocket Recipe: Roast potatoes with rosemary

2–5kg bag (roughly one large potato per head) of King Edward's or Maris Piper potatoes
200ml olive oil (or goose fat, if preferred)
mustard powder
dried thyme
1 sprig of fresh rosemary, leaves stripped and finely chopped

1. Peel the potatoes and cut in half (or quarters for large potatoes). They will roast best if they are all the same size. Then boil in salted water for 5 minutes and drain. Parboiling can be done early on Christmas Day to leave yourself more time.

2. Shake the potatoes in the pan and roughen the surface of each potato with a fork.

3. Pour the oil (or goose fat) into a roasting tray and heat at 220C in the top of the oven for around 5 minutes.

4. Remove the tray from the oven and place the potatoes in the tray, spooning hot oil over the top. Season and sprinkle with mustard powder and rosemary.

5. Roast for around 30 minutes at 220C or until crisp and golden, shaking and turning once.

Don't forget: Christmas Day

- *Preheat oven to 190°C (gas mark 5). Stuff the turkey and put it in the oven.*
- *Prepare, parboil and roast the potatoes.*
- *Put the Christmas pudding on to steam.*
- *Prepare and cook the leeks, sprouts and parsnips.*
- *Make the gravy using the prepared stock and the juices from the roast turkey.*
- *Prepare the pigs in blankets and add to the turkey roasting pan 40 minutes before the end of the turkey's cooking time.*
- *Reheat the bread sauce and add the cream.*

Pocket Recipe: Leeks and Brussels sprouts with toasted almonds

450g sprouts
3 leeks
125g baby sweetcorn

15–25g butter
25g toasted flaked almonds

1. Peel the sprouts, thickly slice the leeks and cut the baby sweetcorns in half lengthways.

2. Bring a large pan of salted water to the boil then toss in the vegetables. Boil for 10 minutes until the veg is tender but still crisp.

3. Pile the veg into a warmed serving dish, add a little butter, season, and sprinkle with the nuts.

Sprout facts

The humble Brussels sprout, with its bitter taste and unappealing aroma, holds the dubious accolade of most hated vegetable in Britain, yet it is routinely served up on Christmas Day in households up and down the country. Why? Because it's traditional. And so it will continue to be denigrated, pushed aside and criticised at Christmas dinners for centuries to come. Let's celebrate it with some sprout facts:

- *The sprout's trademark bitter taste comes from a chemical defence that the clever little sprout has evolved to stop insects from attacking it.*
- *Captain Cook had his crew eat sprouts daily to help combat scurvy.*
- *Sprouts are routinely part of the Christmas dinner because they are allegedly best harvested later in the season after a few sharp frosts, and so were one of the few vegetables in season at Christmas in times gone by.*
- *The superstitious practice of cutting a cross in the base of the sprout was originally designed to keep the Devil out,*

though many cooks will tell you it helps the sprouts to cook evenly. Modern thinking is that crossing may result in a loss of flavour.

- *The Romans used the sprout as an early Berocca. Statesman Cato (234–149 BC), who liked a drink or two, commended them as the best hangover remedy known to man.*
- *Taste sensitivity decreases with age, so sprouts really are more offensive-tasting to children than to adults.*
- *Each October, Chipping Campden in Gloucestershire hosts a sprout festival, inspired by a local chef who invented the sprout cake.*
- *Weight for weight, sprouts contain three times as much vitamin C as oranges.*
- *It's true — sprouts do make you fart! During cooking, sprouts release sulphur compounds, which react with bacteria in the gut to produce hydrogen sulphide, one of the main ingredients of the stink bomb.*

Pocket Recipe: Honey-glazed parsnips

500g bag of medium-size parsnips
4 tbsp olive oil
25g butter
dried thyme
2 tbsp clear honey

1. Top, tail and peel the parsnips, then cut them in half lengthways.

2. Heat the butter and oil in a frying pan and sauté the parsnips, sprinkled lightly with thyme and seasoning for about 10 minutes until tender.

3. Spoon the honey into the pan and stir the parsnips gently to coat. Fry for another few minutes until the parsnips are glazed, and serve. They should be soft and deliciously caramelised.

Alternative Christmas lunch ideas

If you're tired of the traditional Christmas fare, remember it's only the British and North Americans who are such sticklers for the traditional roasted poultry option. Make it a cosmopolitan Christmas and tuck in to some of these alternative menus from around the world:

- **Czech Republic:** Fried carp and potato salad.
- **Finland:** A Joulupöytä – similar to a Swedish smörgasbord of ham, mustard, laatikot (liver and raisin casserole with rice), lutefisk and gravlax (fish).
- **France and Quebec:** A mixture of oysters, lobster, snails, foie gras, turkey stuffed with chestnuts and Tourtiere (pork pie).
- **Iceland:** Hangikjöt or smoked mutton with laufabrau, similar to Welsh lavabread.
- **Jamaica:** Curried goat, stewed oxtail, rice and peas. For dessert, try Jamaican red wine and white rum fruitcake.
- **Latvia:** Lentils or peas with bacon, meat pies, cabbage and sausage.
- **Norway:** Cod with boiled potatoes, washed down with beer and punch.
- **Sweden:** Herring, ham and beans.
- **Greenland:** Kiviak – raw auk meat that has been wrapped in sealskin and buried for several months until suitably decomposed.

What to drink on Christmas Day

On Christmas Day you are unlikely to find yourself re-corking any wine, especially if you have guests. A good tip is to pop into your local independent wine shop and invest in a good magnum or three. Not only does a magnum look great on the Christmas table, but you will get better value for money and be able to invest in a higher quality wine. It's a good idea to get at least one white and one red, and a magnum of Champagne if you're feeling flush.

White wine goes very well with turkey, particularly a Viognier, which provides a refreshing counterpoint to all that heavy food. But most people will want to drink red, so invest in a Beaujolais Cru or a good Syrah. Pinot noir also goes very well with the full turkey dinner. If you're serving goose then try a nice Sauvignon blanc for the white wine drinkers and a Zinfandel or Tempranillo for the rest.

A small bottle of either a Rutherglen Muscat from Australia or a Moscatel sherry will go down extremely well with Christmas pudding and mince pies.

TRIMMINGS

Stuffing, or forcemeat as it was known in the Middle Ages, has long been recognised as a vital component of the Christmas lunch. Not only does it help the turkey or goose maintain its shape during cooking, it also makes the meat go further, and some historians believe that the antiseptic properties of sage, thyme and marjoram helped protect against the effects of off or undercooked poultry. Aside from all this, it's a delicious addition to any Christmas lunch. Try the traditional sausage and apple stuffing recipe below.

Pocket Recipe: Sausage and apple stuffing

(Stuffs a 10–12lb turkey)
1 onion
1 tbsp olive oil
450g pork sausages
50g fresh breadcrumbs
175g Bramley apples
1 tbsp fresh, chopped sage

1. Finely chop the onion and lightly fry in a pan of olive oil until soft.

2. Peel, core and chop the Bramley apples.

3. Remove the sausage skins and place the meat in a bowl with the onion, the breadcrumbs, the chopped apples and the sage. Season with salt and freshly ground black pepper.

4. Mix thoroughly by hand and use to stuff the neck end of the turkey to add flavour and keep the meat moist.

5. Any leftover stuffing can be rolled into balls and cooked in the oven for 30 minutes, then served as a garnish around the turkey.

Pocket Recipe: Luxury pigs in blankets

24 cocktail sausages (or chipolatas)
12 rashers smoked streaky bacon
3 tbsp clear honey
5 drops Tabasco
1 tbsp bourbon

1. Cut each rasher in half horizontally and roll around a sausage. Keep the bacon in place with a cocktail stick if necessary.

2. Mix together the honey with the drops of Tabasco and splash of bourbon. Pour over the sausages, making sure that each sausage is well covered.

3. Remove the turkey from the oven 40 minutes before it's ready and place the sausages around the base. Alternatively, cook them separately on a baking tray (at 180°C) for 40 minutes until piping hot.

Pocket fact ☆

In medieval England it was traditional to serve up a sacrificial boar's head at Christmas feasts. According to folklore, the offering of a boar would lead to good fortune for the coming year, and it was particularly associated with the feast of St Stephen. As a remnant of this tradition, Boar's Head Feasts, complete with a procession and carols, still take place each year at Queen's College, Oxford, and the Stourbridge Old Edwardian Club.

Pocket Recipe: Special gravy

Turkey giblets

1½ pints of water

bay leaves

1 onion

chicken stock cube

2 tbsp port

1 tbsp cornflour

1. Make up some stock with the giblets you removed from the turkey, water, a few bay leaves and an onion. Simmer for an hour, strain and chill until required. This can be done on Christmas Eve to save time on the day.

2. When the turkey is cooked, pour the juices from the roasting tin into a jug and skim the fat from the top.

3. Make the turkey juices up to 425ml with the giblet stock and add in a chicken stock cube. Place in a pan and bring to the boil.

4. Blend in the port and the cornflour and stir until thickened.

5. Season and pour into a gravy boat.

Pocket Recipe: Luxury bread sauce

575ml (1 pint) milk
1 onion
6 cloves
1–2 bay leaves
125g fresh breadcrumbs
25g butter
4 tbsp double cream
salt and freshly ground black pepper

1. Finely chop the onion and heat in a large pan along with the milk, cloves and bay leaves. Part cover and allow to simmer for 30 minutes, or until the onion is soft.

2. Slowly stir in the breadcrumbs, butter and seasoning until smooth.

3. Remove the bay leaves and cloves, reheat if necessary and stir in the cream.

Pocket Recipe: Port and cranberry sauce

350g fresh or frozen cranberries
125g soft brown sugar
75ml ruby port

1. Throw the cranberries in a pan with the sugar and port and heat.

2. Bring to the boil then turn down the heat and cook for about 6–8 minutes, stirring constantly, until the cranberries are tender and form a pulpy sauce.

3. Spoon into a sauceboat to cool, then cover and chill before serving.

Setting the Christmas table

Setting the table for guests at Christmas dinner can be an ordeal, especially as you have so much else to worry about. With so many dishes and guests jostling for position, it's important to keep the table decorations minimal and create a balance between practicalities and attractiveness. Here are some tips to help you get it just right:

- *Personalise the place settings with individual touches. If you have children who are getting under your feet then ask them to draw place cards with the person's name and a little symbol of something that represents that person. Or, if you want to impress, tie a name tag to a colourful bottle or ornament that guests can take away with them.*

- *Before setting the table, think about the practicalities of who should be sitting where, especially who needs to be near the kitchen and who needs to be able to get out easily.*

- *Is there enough room to bring the turkey plate to the table? If not, consider using a separate side table, or serving trolley if you have one, to minimise clutter on the table.*

- *Don't make the decorations too fussy. Two floral arrangements, one at each end of the table, will be simple and effective.*

- *Christmas lunch can become awkward and messy if too many items are being passed up and down the table, so it might be best to have several butter dishes, gravy boats, salt cellars and the like on the table. Alternatively you could consider individual servings of salt and butter at each setting, as long as there is space.*

- *If you are using fresh flowers, remember to add them to the table just before your guests arrive.*

❋ SWEET CHRISTMAS ❋

CHRISTMAS PUDDING

Traditional Christmas pudding needs at least six weeks to mature (see p. 25), which goes some way to explaining why less than 20% of modern families enjoy a homemade Christmas pudding. It has to be said that the shop-bought Christmas pudding tastes pretty good these days. Nevertheless, making your own pudding is fun and an essential part of the truly traditional Christmas. Custom decrees that during the preparation, the whole family must take a hand in stirring the pudding mixture, and each family member gets a secret wish. Stirring *must* be done in a clockwise direction (or from east to west, in honour of the Three Wise Men), with eyes shut, or the wish will not come true.

Pocket fact ☆

We've all heard of finding a silver sixpence in our Christmas pudding, but the Victorians threw all sorts of charms into their puddings, each with a different significance. For example, a ring would bring love to the finder, a trouser button was for the bachelor, a thimble for the spinster, and a tiny pig determined the glutton of the group.

Another tradition suggests that a true Christmas pudding must be made of exactly 13 ingredients, to represent Christ and his 12 disciples. Granted, the recipe below has slightly more ingredients, but you'll still find it pretty tasty.

Pocket Recipe: Traditional Christmas pudding

(NB – you need to start making this at least six weeks before Christmas to allow it to mature)

225g fine soft breadcrumbs
110g plain flour

225g moist brown sugar
225g shredded suet
4 large eggs
225g mixed, candied peel, chopped
450g chopped raisins
225g currants
225g sultanas
110g glacé cherries, chopped
110g cooking apple, peeled and grated
110g carrots, grated
110g blanched almonds, chopped
1 tsp grated lemon rind
1 tsp grated orange rind
1 tsp ground nutmeg
1–2 tsps mixed spice
1 tsp ground cinnamon
1 tbsp black treacle
150ml stout or ale
1 tbsp orange juice
1 tbsp lemon juice
1 wineglass brandy or rum

1. Mix all the ingredients together (remember that the whole family needs to give it a stir and make a wish) and leave it to stand overnight, giving the flavours time to blend together.

2. Grease two 2.5 litre basins and add the mixture. Don't over-fill the basins as the pudding will swell during cooking. Cover well with greased greaseproof paper and foil.

3. Steam each pudding for 6 to 8 hours and then remove the damp covers. Cool the puddings and add dry covers. Store in a cool dry place for six weeks or more.

4. On Christmas morning, steam for another 2–3 hours and then serve.

Pocket fact ☆

The figgy pudding, demanded so brusquely in the carol, We Wish You a Merry Christmas, *is not Christmas pudding at all. Christmas pudding is in fact plum pudding, whereas figgy pudding, enjoyed in Victorian times, has quite a different taste and is white in colour.*

MINCE PIES

Quite unlike the tasty treats we enjoy today, medieval Christmas pies were shaped like Jesus' crib and contained a range of shredded meats (see p. 28), from goose to veal. Today's mince pies may be a different size and shape, but they need be no less lavish, and the ingredients are far tastier:

Pocket Recipe: Rich almond, Guinness and whisky mince pies

Mincemeat ingredients
450g mixed dried fruit
225g chopped, stoned dates
150g dried apricots, chopped
100g large raisins
575g Bramley apples, peeled and grated
1 tsp ground ginger
1 tsp nutmeg
1 tsp cinnamon
440 ml can Guinness
5 tbsp whisky

1. Add all of the ingredients (minus the whisky) to a large saucepan.

2. Bring to the boil, then cover and simmer until the apples are cooked (about 20 minutes), stirring occasionally to stop the mixture from sticking.

3. Cool slightly and then stir in the whisky.

4. Spoon into jars, seal and cool in the fridge until required (it will keep for up to a month).

Pastry ingredients
275g self-raising flour
2 tbsp icing sugar
50g ground almonds
125g butter
50g white vegetable fat
3 tbsp milk
1 egg, beaten
675g mincemeat (use half the recipe above)

Topping ingredients
1 egg, beaten
50g flaked almonds

1. Place the flour, ground almonds, icing sugar and vegetable fat in a bowl. Rub the fat into the ingredients until the mixture resembles breadcrumbs. Beat the milk into the egg, then carefully mix into the dry ingredients.

2. Bring the mixture together to form a soft dough (make sure you don't over-mix as the oil in the almonds can upset the balance of fat to flour).

3. Roll out around two-thirds of the pastry until it is roughly 6mm thick and then use a pastry cutter to cut out as many circles (approx 11cm diameter) as you can.

4. Cut a wedge out of each circle and fit them snugly into deep muffin tins. Chill in the tin for about 10 minutes.

5. Put about a tablespoon of mincemeat into each case. Then use the remaining third of the pastry to cut out smaller circles for

the tops (roughly 7cm diameter). Brush with a little cold water, then place on top of the mincemeat.

6. Lightly pinch the pastry tops and bottoms together to seal them. Brush the beaten egg over the tops to glaze, and sprinkle each with a few glazed almonds.

7. Bake at 200C (gas mark 6) for 10–15 minutes, or until the pastry and almonds are golden brown.

8. Remove from tins and cool on a wire rack. Store in an airtight container.

Pocket fact ☆

An estimated 850 million mince pies are left out for Santa every Christmas Eve.

CHRISTMAS CAKE

Pocket Recipe: Last-minute Christmas cake

Cake ingredients
575g mixed dried fruit
225g sultanas
175g stoned chopped dates
2 lemons
150ml ruby port
225g softened butter
250g plain flour
4 eggs
1 tbsp black treacle
1 tsp ground cinnamon
1 tsp mixed spice
100g pecan nuts
100g blanched hazelnuts
175g glacé cherries

Decoration

4 tbsp apricot jam
675g icing sugar
450g white marzipan
2 egg whites at room temperature
2 tsp glycerine
Juice of half a lemon
1 tbsp brandy
125g silver sugar almonds
Sprig of holly

1. Line a 23cm round, loose-based cake tin with greaseproof paper.

2. Put all of the fruit (minus the cherries) in a large saucepan along with the grated rind and juice of two lemons and the port. Bring to the boil stirring constantly, remove from the heat and stand the pan in a bowl of cold water to cool the fruit quickly.

3. Place the flour, butter, eggs, treacle and spices in a mixing bowl and beat together. Fold in all the fruits and the nuts until well combined. Then stir in the cherries and pour the mixture into the lined cake tin, flattening off the top.

4. Bake at 150C (gas mark 2) for three hours. Insert a skewer into the centre of the cake – if it comes out clean, the cake is ready. Cool overnight in the tin.

5. Turn out the cake and remove the lining paper.

6. For the decoration, heat the jam with 1tbsp water and brush onto the outside of the cake.

7. Roll out a third of the marzipan to fit the top of the cake, trim away the excess and roll the remaining marzipan to fit around the sides. Leave to dry overnight.

8. To make the icing, beat together the egg whites and glycerine. Add half the icing sugar 3 tablespoons at a time, beating well all the time. Then beat in the lemon juice. Continue adding the remaining icing sugar until it forms stiff peaks.

9. Brush the marzipaned cake with the brandy and spread the icing over it with a palette knife.

10. Decorate with almonds and leave overnight. Just before serving, top with a sprig of holly.

YULE LOG

The chocolate Yule log is a firm festive favourite that has its roots far back in history (see p. 36). In France, from around the 12th century, it became customary to ceremoniously bring a Yule log into the house at Christmas time, sprinkle it with oil, salt and mulled wine, and pray around it. It was believed that this ritual would protect the house from evil forces. Around the 18th century, the French created a traditional dessert in honour of this custom, called *bûche de Noël*, which has evolved into the chocolate log we know today.

Pocket Recipe: Chocolate Yule log

Cake ingredients
6 egg yolks
150g white sugar
30g cocoa powder
1½ tsps vanilla extract
6 egg whites
icing sugar for dusting

Filling ingredients
475ml double cream
60g icing sugar
50g cocoa powder
1 tsp vanilla extract

1. Preheat the oven to 190C and line a baking tray (approx 25x38cm) with greaseproof paper.

2. **Filling:** Whip the cream, icing sugar, cocoa and vanilla together in a large mixing bowl until the mixture is thick and stiff. Put the bowl in the fridge.

3. **Cake:** In a separate mixing bowl beat the egg yolks with 100g sugar until thick and pale, then blend in the cocoa, vanilla and a pinch of salt.

4. In a large bowl, whip the egg whites to soft peaks and gradually add the remaining 50g of sugar, and beat until the whites form stiff peaks. Then fold the yolk mixture into the whites and spread the batter evenly into the baking tray and bake for 12–15 minutes.

5. Run a knife around the edge of the baking tray and turn the warm cake onto a clean tea-towel dusted with icing sugar. Remove the greaseproof paper. Roll the cake up with the towel and cool for half an hour.

6. Unroll the cake and spread the filling from the fridge onto it, leaving about an inch gap from the edge of the cake. Roll the cake up with the filling inside and place seam edge down onto a plate. Dust with icing sugar and serve.

ACCOMPANIMENTS

Pocket Recipe: Brandy butter

The perfect accompaniment to Christmas pudding and mince pies is best made a day before serving.

100g unsalted butter
175g icing sugar
3–4 tablespoons brandy
A few glacé cherries
Blanched almonds

1. Cream the butter until soft, sieve in the icing sugar and beat until the mixture is very white.

2. Gradually beat in the brandy.

3. Spoon into the serving dish and decorate with small pieces of cherry and the almonds.

Rum butter

As above but substitute demerara sugar for icing sugar and rum for brandy.

Seasonal fruit and nuts

What better snack is there to offer Christmas guests than a selection of fresh fruit and nuts? Serve a mixture of fresh seasonal fruits such as satsumas, clementines and pomegranates, or even try out some more exotic fruits that are available at this time of year, such as lychees and kumquats. Then add in a variety of nuts in their shells, such as pecans, walnuts, almonds and hazelnuts, all of which are at their best at this time of year.

❄ THE SPIRIT OF CHRISTMAS ❄

Nothing warms the cockles better during the frosty festive season than a glass or two of your favourite seasonal tipple. Why not try a few of these Pocket Recipes? 'Tis the season to be jolly, after all.

Pocket Recipe: Mulled Wine

The British have been mulling since the early Middle Ages, or even further back in time. First appearing in cookbooks in the 16th century, the recipe hasn't changed too much over the years:

1 bottle red wine
60 ml sloe or damson gin
60g demerara sugar

1 cinnamon stick
1 bay leaf
grated nutmeg
8 cloves
2 sliced oranges
1 sliced lemon

1. Pour the wine into a saucepan, along with the sugar, bay leaf, orange and the spices.

2. Heat very gently, stirring all the time, until the sugar has dissolved. Taste to see if you want the wine sweeter, and add more sugar to taste. Do not allow the wine to boil, otherwise the flavour will be spoiled and, even worse, the alcohol will evaporate.

3. Take the pan off the heat and stir in the sloe or damson gin.

4. Strain into heatproof glasses and serve.

Pocket fact ☆

Hippocrates, the Father of Medicine himself, is believed to have invented the first mulled wine recipe. Named Ypocras, it was a popular medieval drink made of wine heated with honey and spices, and it was considered to keep away all ills. Indeed, doctors recommended that it be taken at the end of a meal to aid digestion and maintain good health.

Pocket Recipe: Hot toddy (serves 8–12)

2 thinly sliced fresh lemons
cloves
700 ml whisky
4 tbsps sugar
1 stick cinnamon
4 pints boiling water

1. Stud the lemon slices with three cloves each.

2. Pour the whisky, sugar and cinnamon into a pan and heat gently. When it's on the verge of boiling add the water.

3. Put the spiced lemon slices into mugs and pour the mixture over them.

Pocket fact ☆

Hot toddy is believed to have originated in the 18th century to make the taste of Scotch more palatable to women.

Pocket Recipe: Eggnog (serves 8–12)

6 fresh eggs
6 tablespoons sugar
1 pint milk
350 ml (½ bottle) whisky
230 ml dark rum
1 pint thick cream
grated nutmeg

1. Separate the eggs, putting the whites into a large bowl.

2. Beat the egg yolks until smooth, adding the sugar and half a pint of milk at the same time. Pour this mixture into a punch bowl. Add the whisky, mixing well. Then add the rum.

3. Whip the egg whites until they are stiff.

4. Add the remaining milk and the cream to the punch bowl. Stir together and fold in the egg white.

5. Sprinkle the grated nutmeg on top and serve.

CHRISTMAS CAROLS

Here, we bring you a short history of some of Britain's best-loved Christmas carols . . .

❄ *DING DONG MERRILY ON HIGH* ❄

Based around a 16th-century French folk melody called *Le Branle de l'Official*, this most English of carols was a secular dance tune until English writer and enthusiastic amateur campanologist George Ratcliffe Woodward composed the lyrics in 1924.

Ding dong merrily on high,
In heav'n the bells are ringing:
Ding dong! verily the sky
Is riv'n with angels singing.
Gloria, Hosanna in excelsis!

E'en so here below, below,
Let steeple bells be swungen,
And "Io, io, io!"
By priest and people sungen.
Gloria, Hosanna in excelsis!

Pray you, dutifully prime
Your matin chime, ye ringers;
May you beautifully rime
Your evetime song, ye singers.
Gloria, Hosanna in excelsis!

❊ GOD REST YE MERRY GENTLEMEN ❊

Dating probably from the 15th century, this olde-English classic may well be the most ancient of our Christmas songs. The carol also makes a cameo appearance in Dickens' *A Christmas Carol*, sung by a hapless caroller Scrooge chases from his door.

God rest ye merry, gentlemen
Let nothing you dismay
Remember, Christ, our Saviour
Was born on Christmas Day
To save us all from Satan's power
When we were gone astray
O tidings of comfort and joy,
Comfort and joy
O tidings of comfort and joy

In Bethlehem, in Israel,
This blessed Babe was born
And laid within a manger
Upon this blessed morn
The which His Mother Mary
Did nothing take in scorn
O tidings of comfort and joy,
Comfort and joy
O tidings of comfort and joy

From God our Heavenly Father
A blessed Angel came;
And unto certain Shepherds
Brought tidings of the same:
How that in Bethlehem was born
The Son of God by Name.

O tidings of comfort and joy,
Comfort and joy
O tidings of comfort and joy

'Fear not then,' said the Angel,
'Let nothing you affright,
This day is born a Saviour
Of a pure Virgin bright,
To free all those who trust in Him
From Satan's power and might.'
O tidings of comfort and joy,
Comfort and joy
O tidings of comfort and joy

The shepherds at those tidings
Rejoiced much in mind,
And left their flocks a-feeding
In tempest, storm and wind:
And went to Bethlehem straightway
The Son of God to find.
O tidings of comfort and joy,
Comfort and joy
O tidings of comfort and joy

And when they came to Bethlehem
Where our dear Saviour lay,
They found Him in a manger,
Where oxen feed on hay;
His Mother Mary kneeling down,
Unto the Lord did pray.
O tidings of comfort and joy,
Comfort and joy
O tidings of comfort and joy

Now to the Lord sing praises,
All you within this place,
And with true love and brotherhood
Each other now embrace;
This holy tide of Christmas
All other doth deface.
O tidings of comfort and joy,
Comfort and joy
O tidings of comfort and joy

❄ GOOD KING WENCESLAS ❄

Good King Wenceslas is a pretty unusual carol as the words make no reference whatsoever to the nativity. They were written in 1853 by the infamous Victorian caroller John Mason Neale and set to the tune of a 300-year-old Finnish springtime carol. Sadly the narrative is not based in fact. For a start, Wenceslas was not a king but a duke who took control of Bohemia in the 10th century. He was a controversial leader, and his zealous Christianity was to lead to his downfall. Non-Christian noble factions including his own brother, Boleslav, assassinated him on the way to mass. He was only 22 years old.

Soon afterwards, the funeral reports of miracles taking place at his tomb came thick and fast, until Boleslav, fearful of reprisals from beyond the grave, had his brother's remains moved to Prague. Wenceslas was eventually canonised and made patron saint of Bohemia.

Good King Wenceslas looked out
On the feast of Stephen
When the snow lay round about
Deep and crisp and even
Brightly shone the moon that night
Though the frost was cruel

When a poor man came in sight
Gath'ring winter fuel

'Hither, page, and stand by me
If thou know'st it, telling
Yonder peasant, who is he?
Where and what his dwelling?'
'Sire, he lives a good league hence
Underneath the mountain
Right against the forest fence
By Saint Agnes' fountain.'

'Bring me flesh and bring me wine
Bring me pine logs hither
Thou and I will see him dine
When we bear him thither.'
Page and monarch forth they went
Forth they went together
Through the rude wind's wild lament
And the bitter weather

'Sire, the night is darker now
And the wind blows stronger
Fails my heart, I know not how,
I can go no longer.'
'Mark my footsteps, my good page
Tread thou in them boldly
Thou shalt find the winter's rage
Freeze thy blood less coldly.'

In his master's steps he trod
Where the snow lay dinted
Heat was in the very sod
Which the Saint had printed
Therefore, Christian men, be sure

Wealth or rank possessing
Ye who now will bless the poor
Shall yourselves find blessing

❄ HARK! THE HERALD ANGELS SING ❄

Written by Charles Wesley (younger brother of John Wesley, the
founder of Methodism) and first published in 1739, the tune for
this familiar carol changed several times before finally settling, in
1840, on the Felix Mendelssohn composition we know today.

Hark! the herald angels sing
'Glory to the newborn King!
Peace on earth and mercy mild
God and sinners reconciled.'
Joyful, all ye nations rise
Join the triumph of the skies
With the angelic host proclaim:
'Christ is born in Bethlehem'
Hark! The herald angels sing
'Glory to the newborn King!'

Christ by highest heav'n adored
Christ the everlasting Lord!
Late in time behold Him come
Offspring of a Virgin's womb
Veiled in flesh the Godhead see
Hail the incarnate Deity
Pleased as man with man to dwell
Jesus, our Emmanuel
Hark! The herald angels sing
'Glory to the newborn King!'

Hail the heav'n-born Prince of Peace!
Hail the Son of Righteousness!

Light and life to all He brings
Ris'n with healing in His wings
Mild He lays His glory by
Born that man no more may die
Born to raise the sons of earth
Born to give them second birth
Hark! The herald angels sing
'Glory to the newborn King!'

❄ THE HOLLY AND THE IVY ❄

Composed around 1700, this classic Christmas carol is more correctly classified as a folk song, dealing as it does with ancient English symbols more associated with the Celts than the Christians.

The holly and the ivy,
When they are both full grown
Of all the trees that are in the wood
The holly bears the crown
O the rising of the sun
And the running of the deer
The playing of the merry organ
Sweet singing of the choir

The holly bears a blossom
As white as lily flower
And Mary bore sweet Jesus Christ
To be our sweet Saviour
O the rising of the sun
And the running of the deer
The playing of the merry organ
Sweet singing of the choir

The holly bears a berry
As red as any blood

And Mary bore sweet Jesus Christ
To do poor sinners good
O the rising of the sun
And the running of the deer
The playing of the merry organ
Sweet singing of the choir

The holly bears a prickle
As sharp as any thorn;
And Mary bore sweet Jesus Christ
On Christmas Day in the morn.
O the rising of the sun
And the running of the deer
The playing of the merry organ
Sweet singing of the choir

The holly bears a bark
As bitter as any gall;
And Mary bore sweet Jesus Christ
For to redeem us all.
O the rising of the sun
And the running of the deer
The playing of the merry organ
Sweet singing of the choir

The holly and the ivy
Now both are full well grown,
Of all the trees that are in the wood,
The holly bears the crown.
O the rising of the sun
And the running of the deer
The playing of the merry organ
Sweet singing of the choir

❄ *IN THE BLEAK MIDWINTER* ❄

Probably written around 1872 by English poet Christina Rossetti, this carol did not become popular until after Rossetti's death when the poem was paired with a composition called *Cranham*, by Gustav Holst.

In the bleak midwinter, frosty wind made moan,
Earth stood hard as iron, water like a stone;
Snow had fallen, snow on snow, snow on snow,
In the bleak midwinter, long ago.

Our God, heaven cannot hold Him, nor earth sustain;
Heaven and earth shall flee away when He comes to reign.
In the bleak midwinter a stable place sufficed
The Lord God Almighty, Jesus Christ.

Enough for Him, Whom cherubim, worship night and day,
Breastful of milk, and a mangerful of hay;
Enough for Him, Whom angels fall before,
The ox and ass and camel which adore.

Angels and archangels may have gathered there,
Cherubim and seraphim thronged the air;
But His mother only, in her maiden bliss,
Worshipped the beloved with a kiss.

What can I give Him, poor as I am?
If I were a shepherd, I would bring a lamb;
If I were a Wise Man, I would do my part;
Yet what I can I give Him: give my heart.

❊ *O COME ALL YE FAITHFUL* ❊

Sometimes credited to Handel, the tune for this popular hymn was probably composed by John Francis Wade in 1743. The lyrics, written in Latin, may date back to 13th century Portugal, but of the many translations which have surfaced over the years, the most widespread is the English version, published in Murray's *Hymnal* in 1852.

O come all ye faithful
Joyful and triumphant,
O come ye, O come ye to Bethlehem.
Come and behold Him,
Born the King of Angels;
O come, let us adore Him,
O come, let us adore Him,
O come, let us adore Him,
Christ the Lord.

O Sing, choirs of angels,
Sing in exultation,
Sing all that hear in heaven God's holy word.
Give to our Father glory in the Highest;
O come, let us adore Him,
O come, let us adore Him,
O come, let us adore Him,
Christ the Lord.

All Hail! Lord, we greet Thee,
Born this happy morning,
O Jesus! for evermore be Thy name adored.
Word of the Father, now in flesh appearing;
O come, let us adore Him,
O come, let us adore Him,
O come, let us adore Him,
Christ the Lord.

❋ *SILENT NIGHT* ❋

Surrounded by popular legend, the story has it this carol was quickly written and performed on guitar on Christmas Eve 1818 in Obendorf, Austria, after the church organ stopped working. Whatever the truth of this, the original lyrics for *Stille Nachte* were composed by Father Josef Mohr in 1816 and then set to music by a local headmaster, Franz Xaver Gruber.

Silent night, holy night
All is calm, all is bright
Round yon Virgin Mother and Child
Holy Infant so tender and mild
Sleep in heavenly peace
Sleep in heavenly peace

Silent night, holy night
Shepherds quake at the sight
Glories stream from heaven afar
Heavenly hosts sing Alleluia!
Christ, the Saviour is born
Christ, the Saviour is born

Silent night, holy night
Son of God, love's pure light
Radiant beams from Thy holy face
With the dawn of redeeming grace
Jesus, Lord, at Thy birth
Jesus, Lord, at Thy birth

❄ *TWELVE DAYS OF CHRISTMAS* ❄

Unusual for its lack of religious theme, the version we know today was first printed in 1864, but the repetition of the verses suggest the carol's roots go further back to memory games popular at Twelfth Night celebrations in the 16th century. Popular myth has it that the song is actually a secret catechism, written during a period when Catholicism was banned in the UK, but there is no evidence to support this.

> On the first day of Christmas,
> my true love sent to me
> A partridge in a pear tree.
>
> On the second day of Christmas,
> my true love sent to me
> Two turtle doves,
> And a partridge in a pear tree.
>
> On the third day of Christmas,
> my true love sent to me
> Three French hens,
> Two turtle doves,
> And a partridge in a pear tree.
>
> On the fourth day of Christmas,
> my true love sent to me
> Four calling birds,
> Three French hens,
> Two turtle doves,
> And a partridge in a pear tree.
>
> On the fifth day of Christmas,
> my true love sent to me
> Five golden rings,
> Four . . .

On the sixth day of Christmas,
my true love sent to me
Six geese a-laying,
Five . . .

On the seventh day of Christmas,
my true love sent to me
Seven swans a-swimming,
Six . . .

On the eighth day of Christmas,
my true love sent to me
Eight maids a-milking,
Seven . . .

On the ninth day of Christmas,
my true love sent to me
Nine ladies dancing,
Eight . . .

On the tenth day of Christmas,
my true love sent to me
Ten lords a-leaping,
Nine . . .

On the eleventh day of Christmas,
my true love sent to me
Eleven pipers piping,
Ten . . .

On the twelfth day of Christmas,
my true love sent to me
Twelve drummers drumming,
Eleven . . .

❊ *WE WISH YOU A MERRY CHRISTMAS* ❊

Believed to date from England's west country in the 16th century, this rambunctious carollers' favourite describes the traditional act of going from door to door, singing for Christmas favours. It is also one of the first carols to link Christmas and New Year celebrations.

We wish you a Merry Christmas;
We wish you a Merry Christmas;
We wish you a Merry Christmas and a Happy New Year.
Good tidings we bring to you and your kin;
Good tidings for Christmas and a Happy New Year.

Oh, bring us a figgy pudding;
Oh, bring us a figgy pudding;
Oh, bring us a figgy pudding and a cup of good cheer.
We won't go until we get some;
We won't go until we get some;
We won't go until we get some, so bring some out here.

We wish you a Merry Christmas;
We wish you a Merry Christmas;
We wish you a Merry Christmas and a Happy New Year.

❊ *WHILE SHEPHERDS WATCHED THEIR FLOCKS BY NIGHT* ❊

Written by British poet laureate Nahum Tate during the reign of Queen Anne, the exact date of the composition of this carol is unknown, but the lyrics first appeared in a supplement to the new version of the *Psalms of David* in 1700. Prior to this date only the psalms of David could be sung in the Anglican Church.

While shepherds watched
Their flocks by night
All seated on the ground
The angel of the Lord came down
And glory shone around
And glory shone around

'Fear not,' he said,
For mighty dread
Had seized their troubled minds
'Glad tidings of great joy I bring

To you and all mankind,
To you and all mankind.

'To you in David's
Town this day
Is born of David's line
The Saviour who is Christ the Lord
And this shall be the sign
And this shall be the sign.

'The heavenly Babe
You there shall find
To human view displayed
And meanly wrapped
In swathing bands
And in a manger laid
And in a manger laid.'

Thus spake the seraph,
And forthwith
Appeared a shining throng

Of angels praising God, who thus
Addressed their joyful song
Addressed their joyful song

'All glory be to
God on high
And to the earth be peace;
Goodwill henceforth
From heaven to men
Begin and never cease
Begin and never cease!'

4

MAKE YOUR OWN . . .

❄ HOLLY WREATH ❄

The most traditional of decorations, holly and evergreen wreaths have been part of the Christmas season for longer than Christianity itself.

You will need

1 old coathanger
florist's wire
gardening gloves
1 bag holly with berries
1 bag moss
newspaper
wire cutters
1 red ribbon (about 10 inches)

1. Make the ring

Open out the coathanger and work into a wire circle with your hands. Leave the hook at the top of the circle so you can hang your wreath later.

2. Cover the ring

Wind lengths of rolled newspaper around the wire to cover and thicken the ring and bind in place with florist's wire. Cover the newspaper with a layer of gardening moss (available from florists) and bind in place with florist's wire. A traditional English wreath will also contain ivy so consider winding some into the wreath base now.

3. Make the sprigs

Holly is prickly stuff, so wear your gloves. Select leaves heavy with berries and trim them from the bough, leaving a long stalk. Bind medium-sized bunches of leaves into sprigs using florist's wire and attach sprigs to the wreath ring so they overlap slightly. You will probably need about 20 sprigs to cover the ring. Consider working some mistletoe into your sprigs; remember the wreath is all about the berries.

4. Tie the bow

Take your length of ribbon and attach it to the base of the ring, opposite the hanging hook at the top. Tie the ribbon into a loose bow leaving rings of about four inches either side. Now your wreath is ready to hang.

❄ TABLE CENTREPIECE ❄

Make your Christmas table a feast for the eyes with a simple centrepiece.

You will need

1 circular tray
1 glass tumbler
1 large candle
6 red apples
6 oranges
holly branches
1 cup cranberries

1. Supporting the candle

Place the candle in the glass tumbler and surround with cranberries to hold the candle upright. Place in the centre of the tray and position on your table.

2. Decorating the tray

Surround the tumbler with the apples and oranges, arranging them on the tray and interspersing with holly sprigs and branches. Keep adding holly sprigs and branches until you get the look you are after. Painted pine cones also make good additions.

Pocket tip 🎄

Making the holly branches point towards the candle will give balance to your centrepiece and improve its overall appearance.

❄ TREE DECORATIONS ❄

Personalised Christmas decorations mean so much more than mere baubles.

PINE CONE BAUBLES

- Dry the fresh pine cones overnight in an airing cupboard.

- Place cones on a flat surface, covered with old newspaper, while you spray.

- Hold the nozzle of the spray can about six inches from the cone and apply paint in smooth, even strokes. Always use spray paint in a well-ventilated room.

- Leave to dry for one hour.

- Thread with coloured string or fishing line and hang.

GINGERBREAD TREE HANGINGS

- Make a batch of gingerbread biscuits (see p. 92). These can come in many shapes including Christmas tree, Santa or snowmen.

- Attach the biscuits to lengths of ribbon (about 15cm per biscuit) and hang them from your tree.

POPCORN GARLANDS

Cook up a batch of popcorn and allow to cool.

- Dip individual kernels into coloured food dye – red, green, silver and gold all work well.

- Thread kernels onto string with a needle, alternating between colours.

- Simple but effective, popcorn garlands can be hung from your tree or around the house like streamers.

❄ CHRISTMAS STOCKING ❄

The bigger it is, the more it can hold!

You will need

1 yard of material for each stocking that is to be made, plus ¼-yard material for the stocking cuff (felt is excellent for novices as it does not run easily)

1 tape measure
1 pair sharp fabric scissors
needle and thread
about 20 pins

1. Create your template

Either using an existing Christmas stocking, or a template (there are many available on the internet), cut out two matching, flat stocking shapes to be sewn together. Don't forget to reverse your pattern before cutting the second stocking shape so that the two halves match exactly.

2. Pinning the stocking

Place the two halves of your stocking on top of one another, with the cuffs on the inside. Pin around the two halves together, about ¼ inch in from the rough edges.

3. All sewn up

Using a sewing machine or a needle and thread, sew around the edge of the stocking, remembering to remove the pins as you go. Leave the top of the stocking open or you won't be able to get any presents inside!

4. Attaching the cuff

Using the top of your stocking pattern for length, cut two strips of cuff material 12 inches wide. Measuring six inches in from the top of your stocking, sew the cuff material to the outside of the stocking shape.

5. Reversing the fabric

Turn the stocking inside out and fold down the cuff so the seam remains hidden on the inside. You are now ready to hang your stocking – and hope for the best!

❄ CRACKERS ❄

Cheap, pointless gifts, bad jokes and ill-fitting hats. Who needs commercial crackers anyway?

You will need

empty toilet tissue rolls – 1 for every cracker, plus 1 spare to shape the cracker 'handles'
wrapping paper
glue
scissors
curling ribbon

cracker snaps (available to buy online or in craft shops)
cracker gifts
sweets
hats
jokes

1. Making the barrel

Cut a sheet of wrapping paper to about 25cm by 20cm and roll evenly around one empty toilet roll to create a tube. Seal with glue along the wrapping paper's longest edge.

2. Priming the cracker

If you have cracker snaps, insert one through the centre of the tube and secure with a blob of glue in the handle of the cracker you will seal first. Close this end of the cracker with curling ribbon, ensuring the cracker snap is held in place and that there is enough wrapping paper left over to hold the cracker.

Pocket tip ♔

Insert a second empty toilet roll about half way into the open end of the barrel of your cracker before sealing the cracker. Tie with ribbon between the two cardboard tubes to maintain the clean, round end of your cracker 'handle'.

3. Filling the cracker

Insert your cracker gifts into the open cracker. These can include sweets, hats, jokes, key rings and other small gifts.

4. Sealing the cracker

When your gifts are in place seal the open end of the cracker, as described in Step Two. If you are using cracker snaps, ensure that the free end of the snap passes through the ribbon tie and is pulled tight and secured with glue to both ends of the cracker 'handles'.

5. Ready to go

Using a craft knife or pair of sharp scissors, make perforations in the wrapping paper tube around one of the ribbon tie seals. This will help your cracker break easily when pulled.

❄ ADVENT CALENDAR ❄

Nothing increases the anticipation of Christmas Day more than counting off the days on an advent calendar.

You will need

2 A3 pieces of stiff card
craft knife
glue
ruler
pens, pencils or magazine pictures for decoration

- On one sheet of card draw or paint your calendar design. Christmas trees are popular, as are nativity scenes.

- Over the top of your calendar design, using a ruler, mark out 24 boxes or doors. This is your 'front' calendar panel.

- Using the craft knife cut around three sides of every door, but don't fold them open or they will be difficult to shut again.

- Placing your 'front' calendar panel on top of your second sheet of card, draw squares through the doors of your calendar, onto the 'back' sheet.

- Remove the front sheet and set aside.

- Draw or glue festive pictures into the squares on the back sheet.

- Glue the back sheet firmly behind the front sheet so that when doors are opened they reveal the picture behind.

Pocket tip 🎄

In these days of digital photography making your own Christmas cards has never been easier. Most household printers can print colour photographs to custom sizes, so why not take a family portrait this Christmas, print it on stiff paper card and send to your family and friends — just like the royal family.

❋ GIFT TAGS ❋

For a quick and easy way to save some Christmas cash, make your own gift tags using last year's Christmas cards.

- Choose those cards in which the giver did not write on the back of the card's main image. Luckily, most people only write on the right-hand, inside page of Christmas cards.

- Simply cut out images from the used cards to gift tag size — be creative about the shapes and sizes of your tags.

- Punch a clean hole in a corner of the tag and use either a loop of coloured string or ribbon to attach the tag to your gift.

❋ PRESENTS ❋

For that real personal touch, nothing tops a homemade gift.

CHUTNEY

You will need

1 large, stainless steel saucepan
1 blender
6 x 0.5l sterile jars with screw tops

> *Pocket tip* ⚠
>
> *To sterilise your chutney or jam jars, just put them in the oven on a low heat for 20 minutes.*

500g dried apples
500g dried raisins
500g dried apricots
500g dried, pitted dates
250g brown sugar
600ml water
600ml distilled malt vinegar or white wine vinegar
2 tsp ground ginger
2 tsp ground cinnamon
1/2 tsp ground cloves

- Stir everything into a large saucepan and cover.

- Using a low heat bring to the boil and allow to simmer for 20 minutes, stirring occasionally.

- Leave to cool and then pour into the blender.

- Pulse blend the mix no more than four times; you want a coarse blend for the texture.

- Spoon into the jars and leave for at least three weeks — remember chutney improves with age.

JAM

You will need

1 large saucepan
1kg fresh fruit (berries can be left whole, larger fruits such as apples or peaches should be cut up)
1 kg sugar

half an apple cut into slices
6 x 0.5l sterile jars with screw tops

Pocket tip 🎄

Many people use thickening agents such as pectin in their jam. A few slices of apple, naturally high in pectin, added to your fruit will do the same job.

- Pour the fruit into the saucepan and rough mash it to release the natural juices and pectins.

- Bring the fruit slowly to the boil and remove from the heat.

- Stir in the sugar until it is all completely dissolved.

- Put back onto the heat and boil rapidly for 5 minutes.

- Check the jam is set by scooping some jam onto a fridge-cooled teaspoon. If after one minute the mix has started to crinkle, the jam is cooked. If not, boil it rapidly for a further minute.

- Spoon into airtight jars and seal. Jam can be stored in a darkened cupboard for up to a year.

BEER

You will need
large saucepan
large food-grade bucket with lid and airlock (around 40 litres)
1 metre rubber tubing
1kg sugar
1 thermometer
1 long spoon
sterilising agent
40 pint bottles with caps
1.5kg malt extract

1 tblsp brewer's yeast (a good quality homebrew kit will contain all the equipment and ingredients you will need)

- Sterilise everything: 75% of good home brewing is sanitation. Get it wrong and your homebrew will taste like vinegar.

- Use food-grade sanitiser rather than bleach, which will leave a taste.

- Add around 10 litres of cool tap water to your fermenting bucket. It is worth boiling this water first to kill any bacteria.

- Boil around seven litres of water in your saucepan. Remove from the boil and add your malt extract. Continue to boil for 20 minutes. Congratulations, you have just made wort.

- Remove the wort from the heat and add the sugar, ensuring it is fully dissolved.

- Add the wort to the cold water in the fermenting bucket and top up with fresh water until cool.

- Add the yeast when water is cool to the touch. If the liquid is too hot it will kill the yeast.

- Seal the airtight fermenting bucket and leave for seven days in a warm place (21–27°C is ideal).

- When the bubbles passing through the fermenting bucket's airlock slow to around one bubble every two minutes, primary fermentation is complete and it is safe to start bottling your homebrew.

- Add two teaspoons of sugar to each bottle to kick-start the secondary fermentation process.

- Transfer the brew into bottles using the rubber hose. Be careful not to slosh the beer around too much or the brew will become cloudy with sediment.

- Leave for two weeks in a cool place before drinking.

Pocket tip 🎄

Better quality ingredients make for better tasting beer — invest in good quality brewer's yeast to improve the flavour of your brew.

GINGERBREAD BISCUITS

You will need

2 mixing bowls
1 whisk
flour-dusted cutting and rolling board
rolling pin
festive-shaped cutters
baking tray

To decorate you will need
icing sugar
water
piping bag with fine nozzle

Ingredients

5 cups of flour
1 cup brown sugar
2 large knobs unsalted butter
2 eggs
1 cup molasses
1 tsp ground cinnamon,
1½ tsps baking powder
2 tsps ground ginger
2 tsps ground cloves
1 tsp ground nutmeg
½ tsp salt
2 tbsp water

Makes around 10 pieces.

- Mix the butter and sugar until smooth.

- Add the eggs, molasses and water and whisk.

- Blend the remaining dry ingredients and stir into wet mix until thoroughly absorbed.

- Refrigerate the dough for at least one hour.

- Roll out to about 2.5cm thick and cut biscuits.

- Preheat the oven to 175C/gas mark 4.

- Place biscuits on a greased baking tray, 5cm apart and bake for 11–15 minutes until golden. Not brown!

- When cool decorate your biscuits with icing, piped onto your biscuits. You can also use small sweets, such as Smarties, to add colour to your biscuits.

Pocket fact ☆

The cost of the average unwanted gift in the UK is more than £50.

SPICED OIL

You will need

olive oil
food-safe bottles (preferably with corks)
your choice of herb infusions such as rosemary, chilli pepper, garlic, sage, basil or thyme

- Fresh herbs work better than dried herbs as an infusion.

- Chopped fresh herbs release their flavour to the oil more quickly, but large sprigs look more decorative in a clear bottle.

- The oil needs to stand for at least one week before using.

- There's no reason why you can't combine flavours in an oil, such as garlic and chilli pepper.

- Infusing the oil with lavender or flower petals creates sensual massage oil for a more racy gift.

5

SOCIALISING AND ENTERTAINING

Christmas time is party time, so why not invite guests round to the house when it's sparkling with decorations and Christmas cheer? But with so much else to prepare over Christmas, the last thing you want is to be slaving over a hot stove.

A Christmas party should be fun, and not raise your stress levels through the roof, so keep it simple. An evening gathering with drinks and nibbles is easy to prepare and can be lots of fun, especially if you plan ahead.

Once you have decided who to invite, make lists of everything you need to prepare and plan your food and drink. All you really need are some platters of party food and some good wine. The supermarkets are filled with ready-made canapés and finger food at Christmas time, but guests always appreciate the personal touch. Here are some quick, easy-to-prepare ideas:

❄ PARTY FOOD IDEAS ❄

- Spread cream cheese onto strips of smoked salmon and roll up. Serve on ready-made cocktail blinis or thin toast with lemon and dill.

- Slice French bread or ciabatta and drizzle with olive oil. Top with goat's cheese, cherry tomatoes and thyme and place under the grill. Serve hot.

- Crumble goat's cheese into halved red peppers and drizzle with olive oil. Bake in a medium oven for 20 minutes until the cheese is melted and lightly browned. Divide into quarters and serve.

- Coat cocktail sausages in a glaze of honey and wholegrain mustard. Bake in the oven at 180°C (gas mark 4) for 15 minutes and serve with a sweet chilli dip.

- Pour a bag of tortilla chips onto a baking tray and top with grated cheddar cheese, halved plum tomatoes and olives and bake in a medium oven until the cheese has melted. Serve with soured cream and salsa.

- Dip small strips of plaice in seasoned flour and lightly shallow fry. Serve with tartar sauce.

- Thread cubes of melon and rolled prosciutto onto a cocktail stick and arrange on a platter.

Pocket tip ♤
As a rule of thumb, you should allow eight to 10 canapés per person and a few plates of crisps, nuts, crudités and dips dotted around will help make the food go a bit further.

Preparing your house for guests

- *Don't allow yourself to fret over precious possessions, especially if you're inviting lots of guests. Pack away your prized ornaments and breakables.*
- *Use throws to cover cream sofas or any other furniture that could stain.*
- *Make sure your cleaning materials and dustpan and brush are on hand for any disasters.*
- *Rearrange your furniture so there is a decent-sized space for people to mingle without bumping into your possessions or each other.*
- *Remember to have plenty of napkins on hand for sticky fingers, and liberally scatter coasters around to protect your furniture.*
- *Arrange the food on a large table, preferably with access all the way around it and place smaller satellite tables of nibbles around the room so that your guests aren't falling over each other to get to the grub.*

❄ PARTY DRINKS ❄

It wouldn't be a Christmas party without a little bit of festive spirit, but there's no need to go overboard on the drinks. Remember that many of your guests will bring a bottle or two along, and there's no shame in asking them to do so to help keep costs down. Still it's a good idea to provide around five drinks per person, and most people will expect to drink wine at such a gathering. Don't forget to stock up on soft drinks for the drivers, and make sure you've got plenty of clean glasses.

Pocket tip 🎄

A 750ml bottle of wine will serve five medium-sized glasses.

If you want to add a bit of spice, then there are great recipes for mulled wine, hot toddy and eggnog on p. 62. But for a party, the simplest festive drink to provide is a large bowl of Christmas punch. Try our Pocket Recipe below:

Pocket Recipe: Christmas rum punch (serves 8–10)

30 cloves
3 fresh oranges
175 ml brandy
350 ml dark rum
2 tbsp sugar or sugar syrup
1 bottle cider
cinnamon
ground nutmeg

1. Stick about 10 cloves into each orange and bake them until the rind turns brown.

2. Place the baked oranges into a warmed punch bowl and add the brandy, rum and sugar.

3. Stir the mixture thoroughly and set it alight. Slowly add the cider, putting out the flame.

4. Sprinkle the top with cinnamon and nutmeg. Stir and spoon into punch cups.

Avoiding the Christmas hangover . . .

- **Eat well before you go out.** *Although not good for you on a regular basis, just this once chow down on a fatty meal. Fat is digested slowly and so slows down the absorption of alcohol.*

- **Avoid red wine, port, whisky, brandy or rum.** *These drinks contain high levels of impurities and they give you worse hangovers than say, white wine, gin or vodka.*

- **Alternate your drinks.** *If you have a soft drink between every alcoholic tipple you will keep yourself hydrated and of course drink less. Remember though, fizzy drinks actually speed up the absorption of alcohol into the blood stream, so best to stick to water or fruit juice.*

- **Before bed.** *Walking home, stopping off at the kebab shop is not actually a bad idea. The fresh air and food will help you sober up and stave off some of the hangover, although it would be much better to eat something rich in carbohydrates like a bowl of pasta. Also remember to drink a large glass of water and/or orange juice before bed. Vitamin C helps to speed up the breaking down of alcohol in the body and any liquid will help avoid dehydration.*

❄ CHRISTMAS PARTY GAMES ❄

ADULTS

Snapdragon

From the 16th to the early 20th centuries, no Christmas Eve celebration in England would have been complete without enjoying a game of snapdragon. Involving booze, dim lighting and a hint of danger, Snapdragon is the perfect companion to any Christmas gathering.

Preparation

1. Place 500g of raisins in an old metal pot or bowl. NB the deeper the container you use, the harder the game becomes. Beginners should use a wide, shallow container!

2. Pour cheap whisky or brandy over the raisins (enough to cover them) and leave to soak for at least 24 hours before playing the game.

How to play

When your guests are suitably into the Christmas spirit, set light to the alcohol and dim the lights to make the most of the eerie effect of the blue flame licking at the raisins. The aim of the game is to take it in turns to snatch the raisins out of the bowl and eat them while they are still on fire. If you manage to do this without setting fire to your fingers, face or lounge, then you've won!

Pocket fact ☆

Lewis Carroll's Alice Through the Looking Glass *references this old English Christmas game. The snap-dragon-fly has the body of plum pudding, wings of holly, and a raisin burning in brandy as a head.*

Two truths, one lie

How to play

Everyone makes three statements about themselves, the more outrageous or unbelievable the better. Two of these statements must be true and one of them must be a complete fabrication. The rest of the group can then ask them up to three questions and, on the basis of their answers and what they already know about the person, decide which one of the statements is a lie. A point is earned for each person in the group that incorrectly identifies the lie.

Festive forfeits

Today's forfeits almost always involve downing a shot of something horrible that's been at large at the back of the drinks cabinet for years. But the Victorians were far more creative. These traditional forfeits come from Cassell's Household Guide to Every Department of Practical Life *(c. 1870)*.

For the gentleman

- *Make a Grecian statue. The victim stands on a chair while the group manipulates his limbs into whatever pose they choose.*

- *Choose one of three signs. While the victim is facing the wall, one of the ladies makes three signs in a random order behind his back. The signs are: a kiss, a pinch, and a punch on the ear. The victim may the choose first, second or third, and he receives whichever one he chose.*

- *To kiss the ladies in the room, blindfolded. Of course, once the blindfold goes on the women switch positions with each other and with the men.*

For the lady

- *Kiss a gentleman 'rabbit fashion'. The lady must choose a gentleman and they each put one end of a piece of cotton in their mouths, nibbling towards each other until they are kissing.*

- *Answer 'yes' or 'no' to three questions. While the lady is out of the room, the group decides on what questions to ask. According to Cassell's, 'ladies of experience say the safe answer is always no'.*

- *Kiss each corner of the room. This may sound like the safest option, but those wily gentlemen always immediately pucker up and run to the corners.*

FAMILY

Reverend Crawley's Game

Another excellent Victorian Christmas parlour game, Reverend Crawley's Game is a sort of early Twister, involving gentle exercise and enforced intimacy, with often hilarious consequences. Everyone should give this one a go at Christmas.

How to play

The game works best with large groups (at least eight people). Everyone stands in a circle and links hands – but not with the people on either side, and not both hands with the same person. Once done, you will find that the group has become an enormous human knot and the aim of the game is to untangle yourselves without letting go of the hands you are holding. Working together, you must crawl through gaps, twist around, step over each other, and generally try to wriggle your way out of the mess you've found yourselves in. Your guests will be amazed that, like a magic trick, the knot almost always unties into a single ring of people holding hands in a circle (though occasionally you will get two interlinked rings).

CHILDREN

Pin the nose on the reindeer

This is a festive variation of an old children's classic and very simple to prepare and play.

Preparation

1. Either draw yourself or get the children to draw a picture of a reindeer's head, full size, onto a sheet of A3 paper. Draw an outline for the nose using the compass, but don't complete it.

2. Attach the picture to a wall or flat surface.

3. On the card, draw as many noses as there are children setting the compass to the same diameter as was used on the picture of the reindeer. Cut them out and ask each child to choose a different coloured crayon and colour in their nose.

4. Attach a large blob of Blu-Tack to the back of each nose.

How to play

Ask each child in turn to stand about one to two metres from the picture of the reindeer. Blindfold and spin them round a few times until they are disoriented. Now point them in the direction of the reindeer and tell them to walk forward and stick their nose where they think it should go. The child who is closest to the actual reindeer nose wins.

Hum that carol

How to play

This one works best with large groups. On small pieces of paper write down half as many Christmas songs or carols as you have guests in pairs. Make sure that you write the name of each song out *twice* on separate pieces of paper. Fold the papers up and put them in a hat. Everybody must choose a carol and on the word 'Go' start humming it loudly (warning: this can get quite rowdy!). Each guest must try and locate the person in the room who is humming the same tune. Once they find each other they must raise their hand and start singing the song at the tops of their voices.

6

CHRISTMAS TRIVIA

❄ CHRISTMAS NUMBER ONES SINCE 1970 ❄

Twenty-eight solid gold Christmas hits to get you rocking around the Christmas tree.

Year	Artist	Song	Weeks at No 1
1970	Dave Edmunds	I Hear You Knocking	6
1971	Benny Hill	Ernie (The Fastest Milkman in the West)	4
1972	Little Jimmy Osmond	Long Haired Lover From Liverpool	5
1973	Slade	Merry Xmas Everybody	5
1974	Mud	Lonely This Christmas	4
1975	Queen	Bohemian Rhapsody	9
1976	Johnny Mathis	When A Child Is Born (Soleado)	3
1977	Wings	Mull of Kintyre / Girls' School	9
1978	Boney M	Mary's Boy Child	4
1979	Pink Floyd	Another Brick in the Wall (Part 2)	5
1980	St Winifred's School Choir	There's No One Quite Like Grandma	2
1981	The Human League	Don't You Want Me	5
1982	Renée and Renato	Save Your Love	4
1983	The Flying Pickets	Only You	5

Year	Artist	Song	Weeks at No 1
1984	Band Aid	Do They Know It's Christmas?	5
1985	Shakin' Stevens	Merry Christmas Everyone	2
1986	Jackie Wilson	Reet Petite	4
1987	Pet Shop Boys	Always on My Mind	4
1988	Cliff Richard	Mistletoe and Wine	4
1989	Band Aid II	Do They Know It's Christmas?	3
1990	Cliff Richard	Saviour's Day	1
1991	Queen	Bohemian Rhapsody / These Are the Days of Our Lives	5
1992	Whitney Houston	I Will Always Love You	10
1993	Mr Blobby	Mr Blobby	2
1994	East 17	Stay Another Day	5
1995	Michael Jackson	Earth Song	6
1996	Spice Girls	2 Become 1	3
1997	Spice Girls	Too Much	2
1998	Spice Girls	Goodbye	1
1999	Westlife	I Have A Dream / Seasons in the Sun	4
2000	Bob The Builder	Can We Fix It?	3
2001	Robbie Williams & Nicole Kidman	Somethin' Stupid	3
2002	Girls Aloud	Sound Of The Underground	4
2003	Michael Andrews & Gary Jules	Mad World	3
2004	Band Aid 20	Do They Know It's Christmas?	4
2005	Shayne Ward	That's My Goal	4
2006	Leona Lewis	A Moment Like This	4
2007	Leon Jackson	When You Believe	3
2008	Alexandra Burke	Hallelujah	3

❉ TOP-SELLING TOYS SINCE 1990 ❉

Ever owned a Furby? Remember POGS? Then you were probably a kid (or parent) in the 1990s. Revel in the nostalgia of the best-selling Christmas toys of the past 20 years.

Year	Toy	Description	Maker
1990	Teenage Mutant Ninja Turtles	Cowabunga! We all went pizza crazy for Turtle Power	Bandai
1991	Nintendo Game Boy	Finger-flicking good for the nimble digit generation	Nintendo
1992	WWF Wrestlers	Figures of large, make-up wearing men	Hasbro
1993	Thunderbirds Tracey Island	In fact the real demand for this retro-resurrection was in 1992, but acute shortages meant many were left disappointed	Vivid Imaginations
1994	Power Rangers	From the popular TV show, these brightly coloured heroes karate kick their way to victory.	Bandai
1995	POGS	A game that produced a whole new language. Slam frizz anyone?	Waddingtons
1996	Barbie	The return of the blonde bombshell	Mattel
1997	Teletubbies	They ate custard, spoke gibberish, lived underground and we loved them	Ragdoll Ltd
1998	Furby	The year we all learned Furbish to communicate with our kids	Tiger Electronics
1999	Furby Babies	Smaller, cuter and more coherent than their parents perhaps, but the next generation just couldn't dance	Tiger Electronics

Year	Toy	Description	Maker
2000	Teksta	The robo-pet dog that you still had to spend hours training	Vivid Imaginations
2001	Lego Bionicle	The next generation of Lego, for the next generation of Lego addicts	Lego
2002	Beyblades	Erm. . . it's a spinning top	Hasbro
2003	Beyblades		Hasbro
2004	Robosapien	The robotic friend that walks, throws and dances (a bit)	Wow Wee
2005	Tamagotchi Connection	A bit like portable Facebook – make new friends wherever you go but only ever interact virtually	Hasbro
2006	Dr Who Cyberman Mask	The changing face of Dr Who	Character Group
2007	In the Night Garden Blanket Time Igglepiggle	It sings, it dances and has the oddest name of any toy in history	Hasbro
2008	Ben 10	A whole world in a watch that doesn't seem to tell the time	Bandai

❄ WHITE CHRISTMASES SINCE 1900 ❄

Forget the Christmas card image, according to the Met Office, the standard definition for a White Christmas is for a single snowflake (perhaps amongst a shower of rain and snow mixed) to be observed falling in the 24 hours of 25 December.

There have been 35 officially recorded White Christmases in the UK since 1900, however until 1918 records were only maintained in London – where a snowflake has to be observed falling on the roof of Buckingham Palace for it to qualify.

Official Met Office records are kept at nine locations around the UK:

- London – 10 since records began in 1900

- Birmingham – nine since records began in 1940

- Glasgow – 10 since records began in 1918

- Aberdeen – 15 since records began in 1942

- Aberporth – five since records began in 1941

- Bradford – five since records began in 1971

- Belfast – 11 since records began in 1927

- Lerwick – 19 since records began in 1957

- Newquay (St Mawgan) – five since records began in 1957

Year	Confirmed at	Snow/Sleet Falling	Snow Lying
1916	London	Snow/Sleet	No
1923	Glasgow	Snow	Yes (Glasgow)
1925	Glasgow	Snow	Yes (Glasgow)
1927	London, Glasgow, Belfast	Snow	Yes (London)
1938	London	Snow/Sleet	Yes (London, Glasgow)
1950	Birmingham	Snow	No
1953	Aberdeen	Snow/Sleet	No
1954	Aberdeen	Snow	No
1956	London, Birmingham, Aberdeen, Aberporth, Belfast	Snow	Yes (Birmingham)
1957	Lerwick	Snow/Sleet	No
1960	Lerwick	Snow/Sleet	No
1961	Aberdeen, Lerwick, St Mawgan	Snow	No
1962	Glasgow, Lerwick	Snow/Sleet	Yes (Glasgow)
1963	Glasgow, Aberdeen, Belfast	Snow/Sleet	Yes (Glasgow, Aberdeen, Belfast)
1964	London, Aberdeen, Aberporth, Belfast, Lerwick, St Mawgan	Snow	Yes (Glasgow, Aberdeen, Aberporth, Belfast, Lerwick)

Year	Confirmed at	Snow/Sleet Falling	Snow Lying
1965	Aberdeen, Belfast, Lerwick	Snow/Sleet	Yes (Lerwick)
1966	Aberdeen, Lerwick	Snow	Yes (Glasgow, Lerwick)
1968	London, Birmingham, Aberdeen, Belfast, Lerwick	Snow/Sleet	Yes (Birmingham, Belfast)
1970	London, Birmingham, Glasgow, Aberporth	Snow	Yes (London, Birmingham)
1974	Lerwick	Snow/Sleet	No
1976	London, Aberdeen	Snow	No
1978	Lerwick	Snow	No
1980	Glasgow, Bradford, Belfast	Snow/Sleet	Yes (Glasgow)
1981	London, Birmingham, Aberdeen, Lerwick	Yes (Lerwick)	Yes (Aberdeen, Lerwick)
1985	Lerwick	Snow	No
1988	Lerwick	Snow	No
1990	St Mawgan	Snow/Sleet	No
1993	Aberdeen, Aberporth, Bradford, Belfast, Lerwick	Snow	Yes (Aberdeen, Aberporth, Lerwick)
1995	Aberdeen, Aberporth, Bradford, Belfast, Lerwick	Snow	Yes (Glasgow, Aberdeen, Belfast, Lerwick)
1996	London	Snow/Sleet	No
1998	Belfast	Snow/Sleet	No
1999	London, Birmingham, Glasgow, Bradford, Belfast	Snow/Sleet	No
2000	Birmingham, Glasgow, Aberdeen, Bradford, Lerwick, St Mawgan	Snow	No
2001	Lerwick	Snow	No
2004	Birmingham, Aberdeen, Bradford, Belfast, Lerwick, St Mawgan	Snow	Yes (Lerwick)

CELEBRITIES BORN ON CHRISTMAS DAY

Spot the well-known individuals who only get one set of presents every year.

Alannah Miles. 1958 – Canadian singer songwriter.
Best known for her global hit, *Black Velvet* in 1990.

Annie Lennox. 1954 – British singer/songwriter.
The ex-Eurythmics vocalist, voted by *Rolling Stone* magazine as one of the greatest singers of all time, Lennox has sold over 80 million records worldwide.

Bob James. 1939 – American Jazz musician.
Composer of the now-legendary *Taxi* TV theme tune. The melody is actually called *Angela*.

Humphrey Bogart. 1899–1957 – American actor.
Ranked by the American Film Institute in 1999 as the greatest American actor of all time, Bogie is a full-blown cultural icon.

Ismail Merchant. 1936–2005 – Indian film producer.
Best known for his long-running collaboration with Merchant Ivory films on productions including *The Remains of the Day* and *A Room with a View*.

Noel Langley. 1911–1980 – American playwright, novelist and screenwriter.
Langley is best known as one of the writers who worked on *The Wizard of Oz*.

Noel Hogan. 1971 – Irish guitarist for The Cranberries.
Guitar player and main co-writer for The Cranberries, best known for their hit, *Zombie*, in 1994.

Noel Redding. 1945–2003 – bass guitarist Jimi Hendrix Experience.
British-born bass player Redding featured on Hendrix's seminal albums *Are You Experienced?* (1967), *Axis: Bold as Love* (1968) and *Electric Ladyland* (1968).

Quentin Crisp. 1908–1999 – British writer and actor.
Born Denis Charles Pratt, his 1970 memoir, *The Naked Civil Servant*
made Crisp a gay icon.

Sir Isaac Newton. 1642–1712 – British scientist.
Physicist, mathematician and natural philosopher, Newton's
Philosophiæ Naturalis Principia Mathematica, published in 1687,
remains one of the most influential books of modern science.

Dido. 1971 – British singer/songwriter.
Named after the mythical Queen of Carthage, Florian Cloud de
Bounevialle Armstrong now goes by the nickname Dido.

❄ CHRISTMAS JOKES ❄

That's a cracker! A selection of festive funnies to keep the
Christmas spirit high.

Q. How does Good King Wenceslas like his pizzas?
A. Deep pan, crisp and even!

Q. What's the most common wine at Christmas?
A. Do I have to have the Brussels sprouts?!

Q. What do you call someone who doesn't believe in Father
Christmas?
A. A rebel without a Claus!

- It was Christmas Eve in a supermarket and a woman was
anxiously picking over the last few remaining turkeys in the
hope of finding a large one.
In desperation she called over a shop assistant and said,
'Excuse me. Do these turkeys get any bigger?'
'No,' he replied, 'they're all dead.'

Q. Why does Santa wear pink underwear?
A. He's a man. He did all his laundry in one load.

- The Three Wise Men arrived to visit the child lying in the manger. One of the wise men was exceptionally tall and bumped his head on the low doorway as he entered the stable. 'Jesus Christ!' he shouted.
Joseph said, 'Write that down, Mary. It's better than Clyde!'

Q. Why was Santa's little helper depressed?
A. Because he had low elf esteem.

Q. What do you call Santa's helpers?
A. Subordinate Clauses.

Q. Which reindeer can jump higher than a house?
A. They all can. Houses can't jump!

Q. Why is Christmas just like a day at the office?
A. You do all the work and the fat guy in the suit gets all the credit.

- 'We had grandma for Christmas dinner.'
'Really? We had turkey!'

❊ A CHRISTMAS GRACE ❊

A 19th-century Christmas Day grace by famous atheist and novelist Robert Louis Stevenson:

'Loving Father, Help us remember the birth of Jesus, that we may share in the song of angels, the gladness of the shepherds, and the worship of the wise men. Close the door of hate and open the door of love all over the world. Let kindness come with every gift and good desires with every greeting.

'Deliver us from evil by the blessing which Christ brings, and teach us to be merry with clean hearts. May the Christmas morning make us happy to be Thy children, and the Christmas evening bring us to our beds with grateful thoughts, forgiving and forgiven, for Jesus' sake, Amen.'

❄ ICONIC CHRISTMAS FILMS ❄

It just wouldn't be Christmas without them. The top 10 films we love to see, again and again.

Scrooged, 1988
Great take on the Dickens staple, with Bill Murray as a self-obsessed TV executive haunted by spirits who want him to learn something on Christmas Eve.

It's a Wonderful Life, 1943
Perennial weepy starring James Stuart as a man who is shown just what life would be like if he had never been born.

The Nightmare Before Christmas, 1993
Tim Burton's mystical and ghoulish animated horror. An antidote to any excess of festive sentimentality.

The Muppet Christmas Carol, 1992
Michael Caine acts his heart out to a supporting cast of furry puppets. This is what family entertainment should always be about.

Trading Places, 1983
Off-beat comedy starring Dan Aykroyd and Eddie Murphy about how easily life can turn around.

The Snowman, 1982
Springboard for the career of one Aled Jones on its release, *The Snowman* was directed by Dianne Jackson, also responsible for the harrowing nuclear war animation, *When the Wind Blows*.

The Sound of Music, 1965
Julie Andrews shakes out her nun's habit to great effect in perhaps the most frequently watched Christmas classic in history.

Home Alone, 1990
Macaulay Culkin's family take off for Christmas, not realising that they have left him behind to face a couple of bungling burglars.

A Christmas Story, 1983

How Christmas was in the 1940s, if you were nine. Touching and funny post-lunch fare.

White Christmas, 1954

Bing Crosby and Danny Kaye team up to save a failing Vermont ski inn, using just the power of song and dance.

❄ CHRISTMAS LITERATURE ❄

Find a new Christmas story from these books of the season.

Anton Chekhov – *At Christmas Time* (1900)

Among the last stories completed by Chekhov, *At Christmas Time* is a six-page short story of isolation and loneliness in the festive season.

Charles Dickens – *A Christmas Carol* (1843)

Christmas-hating miser Ebenezer Scrooge is taken on a Christmas Eve journey of redemption by the ghosts of Christmas past, Christmas present and Christmas future.

Charles C Moore – *The Night Before Christmas* (1823)

Perhaps the most famous Christmas poem of all time, it is said to have been composed by Moore on Christmas Eve 1822 to entertain his family, but he did not publicly acknowledge authorship for 15 years.

Dr Seuss – *How The Grinch Stole Christmas* (1957)

Classic American children's story about a cave-dwelling creature with a heart 'two sizes too small' who steals Christmas from the Whos of Whoville.

John Grisham – *Skipping Christmas* (2001)

When Luther and Nora Krank decide to spend a year away from the hassles of the Christmas season, they find they have a whole new set of problems to face.

Kenneth Grahame – *The Wind in the Willows* (1908)
Though not technically a Christmas story, the book's action is set around the Christmas period and Chapter 5, *Dolce Domum* can be read as a retelling of the Christmas story.

Louisa May Alcott – *Little Women* (1868)
This semi-autobiographical tale of growing up with sisters opens with the line 'Christmas won't be Christmas without any presents'.

Raymond Briggs – *The Snowman* (1978)
This completely wordless, children's picture book has become one of the most touching Christmas tales of all time.

Valentine Davies – *Miracle on 34th Street* (1947)
The story of Kris Kringle, a New Yorker obsessed with the idea that he is the real Santa Claus.

William Shakespeare – *Twelfth Night* (1601)
The bard's classic Yuletide romp is a tale of mistaken identity, misrule and love set in the ancient Adriatic region of Illyria.

❄ CHRISTMAS QUIZ ❄

You've read the book, now test your knowledge with the Christmas Trivia Quiz.

Q. George Frideric Handel's great Christmas oratorio, *Messiah*, was first performed in 1742. In what city did the performance take place?
A. Dublin

Q. In *A Christmas Carol*, what song does the caroller sing outside Scrooge's office?
A. *God Rest Ye Merry Gentlemen*

Q. The poinsettia is a traditional Christmas plant. Where did it originally grow?
A. Mexico

Q. What annual Christmas event began in the United Kingdom in 1932?
A. Christmas Day royal address

Q. Who wrote the British monarch's first Christmas Day address?
A. Rudyard Kipling

Q. Which monarch delivered it?
A. George V

Q. In Tchaikovsky's ballet *The Nutcracker*, who is the nutcracker's main enemy?
A. The King of the Mice

Q. How does the ballet's heroine, Clara, finally defeat him?
A. Stuns him with a shoe

Q. Which is the last ghost to approach Scrooge in *A Christmas Carol*?
A. The Ghost of Christmas Yet to Come

Q. And the first?
A. Jacob Marley

Q. What is the biggest selling Christmas single of all time?
A. *White Christmas*

Q. Who wrote it?
A. Irving Berlin, 1942

Q. Which year did the UK public give Mr Blobby the number 1 Christmas single?
A. 1993

Q. How many gifts would you receive if you received all of the gifts in the song *The Twelve Days of Christmas*?
A. 364

Q. How many drummers drumming are there?
A. 12

Q. 26 December, also known as Boxing Day, is the holy day of which saint?
A. St Stephen

Q. Which well known actor died on Christmas Day in 1977?
A. Charlie Chaplin

Q. The real St Nicholas was born in what modern-day country?
A. Turkey

Q. Who introduced the idea of Mrs Claus to Christmas?
A. Katherine Lee Bates in 1889's *Goody Santa Claus on a Sleigh Ride*

7

CHRISTIAN CHRISTMAS

In the rush and melée of modern Christmas it is very easy to forget the true reason for the season. For more than 2,000 years Christians have been gathering at this time to celebrate the birth of Jesus Christ, and thanks to them we have most of our modern traditions. Here are just a few.

❄ RELIGIOUS DATES ❄

ADVENT

If you simply went by the eponymous calendars, you could be forgiven for thinking that advent begins on 1 December. In fact the period covers the four Sundays preceding Christmas Eve and also marks the beginning of the new liturgical year for the western Christian church. Advent officially begins on Advent Sunday (the closest Sunday to the feast of St Andrew the Apostle, 30 November) and lasts until sundown on Christmas Eve. This can place Advent Sunday anywhere between 27 November and 3 December.

For the very early church, the focus of the advent season was more the baptism of Christ, rather than his birth, and this was celebrated on 6 January (modern Epiphany) often with multiple baptisms of new Christians.

Pocket fact ☆

Carol singing traditionally takes place after the third Sunday in advent, which is variously known as Shepherd's Sunday, Gaudete or Joy Sunday.

Traditionally a time of fasting and meditation as strict as Lent, the word advent is derived from the Latin, *adventus* – literally 'the coming' and in the Christian church the period is a time for reflection and preparation.

NATIVITY

Although Christmas Day should be more properly referred to by its official name, the Feast of the Nativity of Christ, very little is actually known about the circumstances of the Feast of the Nativity of Christ (Christmas' official name and Jesus' birthday).

In the bible, the two sources for the nativity come from the Gospel of Matthew and the Gospel of Luke. Although both were probably written within the first century AD, these accounts differ substantially on the details. While both set the birth in Bethlehem, it is from Matthew that we get the story of the magi (three kings) and Luke introduces the manger and shepherds with their flocks.

The colour purple

Also associated with Lent and the crucifixion, the colour purple plays a large part in the Christian advent tradition.

- *Associated with both penance and death, this gloomy shade is primarily used to decorate churches (and clergy) throughout the advent period, reminding congregations that Christ both lived and died for them.*
- *An advent wreath should contain four candles – three purple and one rose. Purple was also a colour associated with royalty and it is said that the purple candles remind us of the coming of the Prince of Peace. The rose candle, lit on the third Sunday of advent (Gaudete Sunday) symbolises joy and celebration.*
- *Some Anglican and Lutheran churches prefer to use blue and not purple in their celebrations, associating blue more closely with the Virgin Mary.*

These discrepancies have led some scholars to suggest that the whole nativity was a later invention by the early church in order to have Christ's birth answer some Old Testament prophecies, including Isaiah 11, that he was of David's lineage; Isaiah 7, which describes the virgin birth; and Micah 5 which predicts Bethlehem as the Messiah's birthplace.

The nativity scene as we know it today didn't really assume its proper place at the Christmas table until the 13th century when St Francis of Assisi popularised the custom of nativity scenes, which by then included not only magi and shepherds, but also angels and animals like the ass, ox, lamb and camel.

EPIPHANY

Epiphany celebrates the arrival of the magi (three kings) to Bethlehem. First mentioned in church records in AD361, the name is derived from the Greek, meaning 'to manifest' or 'to show'. Epiphany's date is fixed on 6 January (although some confusion around switching to the Gregorian calendar in the 13th century means that some traditions celebrate on 19 January). The festival is also sometimes known as Theophany.

Traditionally the day on which gifts were given, remnants of this custom continue today in Italy in the form of the Good Witch, La Befana (Epiphana), who delivers gifts on this date (see p. 127).

Pocket fact ☆

The three kings we know today, Caspar (also Gaspar), Melchior and Balthasar, have only been popular since the sixth century. In the earlier, Syrian tradition, their names were the far more Persian Larvandad, Gushnasaph and Hormisdas.

Epiphany also marks the last of the Twelve Days of Christmas and the close of the festive season. In modern times, 6 January has also become the time many western families take down their Christmas decorations. In the Christian church it has also been the custom to announce the coming dates for Easter at Epiphany services.

CHRISTMASTIDE OR THE TWELVE DAYS OF CHRISTMAS

Christmastide lasts from Christmas Day until 6 January (Epiphany). Introduced in AD567, Christmastide became a way for the Christian church to bridge the divide between the western church's celebration of Christmas Day and the eastern church's veneration of Christ's baptism (6 January, Epiphany). Over time these became known as the Twelve Days of Christmas.

The Twelve Days of Christmas

1st *Feast of St Stephen, First Martyr (26 December)*

2nd *Feast of St John, Apostle and Evangelist (27 December)*

3rd *Feast of the Holy Innocents (28 December)*

4th *Feast of St Thomas Becket Bishop and Martyr (29 December)*

5th *Feast of the Holy Family (first Sunday after Christmas Day)*

6th *Seventh Day in the Octave of Christmas, Feast of St Sylvester (31 December)*

7th *Solemnity of the Blessed Virgin Mary, the Mother of God and the Feast of the circumcision of the Lord (1 January)*

8th *Octave day of St Stephen and saints day for Basil the Great and Gregory of Nazianzen (2 January)*

9th *Octave Day St John (3 January)*

10th *Octave Day Holy Innocents and saint's day for St Elizabeth Ann Seton (4 January).*

11th *St John Neumann (5 January). The night before Epiphany is also known as Twelfth Night.*

12th *The Epiphany of the Lord: Christ is revealed to the magi and is baptised.*

❄ RELIGIOUS SERVICES ❄

CHRISTINGLE

Traditionally held on the last Sunday before Christmas Day, or Christmas Eve, the Christingle service is primarily aimed at children and families.

The first recorded Christingle service took place in Marienborn, Germany, on Christmas Eve in 1747 and the familiar, orange-based decoration we know today was the invention of Moravian pastor Johannes De Watteville. It is said he was trying to find a way to make the Christmas message interesting to children.

Meaning 'Christ light', a Christingle usually takes the form of an orange (representing the world), tied with a red ribbon (the blood of Christ), skewered with four cocktail sticks of sweets and dried fruits (representing the four seasons and God's gifts) and topped by a lighted candle representing Jesus, the Light of the World.

The custom reached the UK in 1968 when it was introduced to the Church of England by the Children's Society. On the 40th anniversary of the Christingle in the UK (2008/9) more than 6,000 Christingle services for the Children's Society took place, raising over £1m for the charity.

CAROL SERVICES

The custom of singing Christmas carols in church was largely frowned upon through the Middle Ages and, as Latin was not understood by Europe's hoi polloi, the popularity of the traditional Christmas masses waned. St Francis of Assisi is credited with returning carols to Christmas Eve at a service in Umbria, Italy, in 1223, which also included the first nativity scene (see p. 120).

The singing of carols was not really accepted by the Church of England until 1880 when Edward White Benson, later Archbishop of Canterbury, drew up the order of Nine Lessons and Carols for use in Truro, Cornwall, on Christmas Eve in an attempt to keep people out of the pubs.

Today, carol services generally take place after the third Sunday in Advent (Gaudete Sunday) and in the UK, while the Church of

England is not compelled to hold services on Christmas Eve, most Anglican churches do and for millions around the world Christmas begins with the service of Nine Lessons and Carols broadcast from King's College, Cambridge.

MIDNIGHT MASS

Midnight Mass is the first mass of Christmas Day in the Catholic tradition. The Anglican equivalent should be referred to as Midnight Communion, but mass has become interchangeable. The one we all know and enjoy singing at, however, is actually the vigil before the Nativity Feast of Christmas Day.

After the fourth century, when Christmas Day became more widely accepted as 25 December, Midnight Masses start to appear across the Christian world and from AD430, Pope Sixtus III established an annual Christmas Eve Midnight Mass at the newly completed basilica of St Mary Major in Rome, in a replica of the cave in which Jesus was said to have been born.

CHRISTMAS DAY

Until the Middle Ages, church attendance was pretty much com-pulsory across western Europe and most people would have attended mass at least once on Christmas Day. For the faithful there were three different services to choose from – or four, if you count the Christmas Eve vigil.

The custom of Christmas Day services was probably imported to England with the Norman conquests and William I was crowned king on Christmas Day 1066. Church attendance was expected and records were kept. The anniversary of Christ's birth is still a Day of Obligation for Catholics.

Pocket fact ☆

The term Cristes Maesse was first recorded by the Church in 1038.

Recent years have seen healthy church attendance during the Christmas season, with an estimated three million people attending church services of all denominations in the UK.

❄ WHY IS CHRISTMAS DAY CELEBRATED ON 25 DECEMBER? ❄

The truth is that nobody is really sure when Jesus was born. By the time the Christian Church had decided that the birth of Christ was something to celebrate, it was hundreds of years after the event, and no one could quite remember the date.

The bible itself actually offers no real clues to the time of year and for early Roman Christians the spring months were most likely candidates. Dates ranging from 21 March to 20 May all found support.

When the Church finally did decide on a date, it was for fairly spurious reasons. Many Christians during the third century believed that the conception of Christ had occurred at the spring equinox, then believed to be 25 March. Count nine months on and you get to the date we know as Christmas today. This suited the Romans nicely, as it was slap bang in the middle of a host of other celebrations. Early church records start to show Christmas Day celebrated on 25 December during the fourth century after Constantine the Great became the first Christian Roman Emperor.

Pre-Christian Christmases

- **Mithra.** Early Christianity's main competitor for the hearts and minds of Europe, Mithra is an Indo-Iranian sun god from ancient Persia. Sharing many characteristics and symbolism with early Christianity, Mithra also had a cult following among soldiers throughout the Roman Empire as the god of manliness and bravery.

- **Yuletide.** The Norse midwinter festival to honour Odin followed the winter solstice (21–25 December in the Julian Calendar) and directly brings us the modern day Christmas traditions of the Yule log (see p. 36), Christmas trees (see p. 31) and many natural decorations. The central ritual involved the burning of a huge log over a period of up to 12 days to scare away the darkness of winter.

- **Saturnalia.** This ancient Roman feast to honour a sun god Saturn, gradually extended to last for a full week, starting from 17 December and running until 24 December. As with most winter festivals, the themes of Saturnalia were chasing away darkness and returning to lighter, more plentiful days. The general feasting was accompanied by gift-giving and misrule when slaves became masters for controlled periods of time.

- **Sol Invictus.** As the name might suggest, another sun god, this time associated with the Roman god Janus. Sol grew in importance in the late Roman period when he was adopted by Emperor Aurelian around 274 as the state's official sun god. His feast day was set on 25 December.

Pocket fact ☆

Orthodox Christians around the world continue to celebrate Christmas on 7 January, particularly in Russia, Armenia and Greece.

❄ FOLK TRADITIONS FROM THE CHRISTMAS STORY ❄

In **Italy**, gifts are traditionally delivered by La Befana, a kindly witch who flies down the chimney on her broomstick to deliver toys to children. The story goes that La Befana was sweeping her floors when the magi stopped at her house and asked her to accompany them to visit the newborn baby Jesus. Weighed down by the pressures of household chores, she declined, but was later racked with regret. To make amends, she has spent every year since searching for the baby Jesus and leaving gifts in every household.

In **Russia**, the story of Babushka (which translates as grandmother) is surprisingly similar. Babushka was visited by the magi, but was equally encumbered with housework (clearly a common problem in the year AD0) and declined to accompany them to Israel. Babushka exists alongside the popular figure of Ded Moroz or Grandfather Frost.

In **Scandinavia** presents are delivered by a gnome called Julenisse who lives in stables or attics. A version of St Nicholas, Julenisse brings good luck and protects the home, but can also become mischievous if not left a bowl of rice pudding for the 12 days of Christmas.

8

CHRISTMAS IN CONTEXT

Christmas is celebrated in about 800 million homes around the world each year. But the customs associated with the season are far from uniform. Festive traditions have built up over time, incorporating older pagan customs, historical events and cultural conventions.

❄ CHRISTMAS THROUGH THE AGES ❄

THE FIRST CHRISTMAS

People did not celebrate Jesus' birthday for quite some time. Early Christian Church leaders considered it sinful to commemorate his birth, as this implied he was a mere mortal. So the first record we have of Christmas being officially celebrated comes from Rome as late as 336AD.

Nevertheless, many of the festivities associated with Christmas can be traced back to thousands of years *before* the birth of Christ. Winter solstice celebrations in Mesopotamia (now Iraq) included 12 days of carousing, lighting fires and giving presents.

The Romans had their own winter festival (from 17 to 24 December) dedicated to Saturn. Saturnalia was a time of overeating, gift-giving, visiting friends and drinking far too much. Astoundingly similar to modern-day traditions, then. They even decorated their homes with candles and branches of evergreen trees.

Pocket fact ☆

For the Romans, 25 December (the day after the end of Saturnalia) was the most important day of the year. It represented the sun at its lowest ebb, the point from which the days began to get longer, and as such it was celebrated as the rebirth or resurrection of the sun. It was known by the Latin name natalis *(birth), from which came the English word nativity.*

Some historians have argued that the Christian Church chose 25 December as the date for Christmas (some time in the fourth century AD) to create a smooth transition from a celebration of the birth of the sun, to a celebration of the birth of the Son of God.

EARLY MODERN CHRISTMAS

It was not until the Christmas Day coronation of William the Conqueror in 1066 that the grand Christmas feasts of the Middle Ages began to take shape. The Norman kings enjoyed hunting wild boar over the festive season and Henry II in particular was a huge fan of over-indulging on Christmas Day, holding decadent feasts lasting up to nine hours, complete with ale and cider mixed with spices.

From the 14th to the 16th century, Christmas at court became a sumptuous affair complete with banquets of swan, heron and peacock, nativity plays, great tournaments and masques. Though not quite so extravagant, these festivities trickled down to the lower classes who would have feasted on simpler fare. Landowners were encouraged to open their houses to tenants and others of a lower social rank to join in the eating, drinking and general merriment.

Pocket fact ☆

The tradition of playing games at Christmas is not as modern as you might think. During the reigns of Henry VI and VII, card playing became an important part of the Christmas celebrations, even though it was banned for the rest of the year. Elizabeth I's favourite Christmas pastime was playing dice, and she was very good at it by all accounts (possibly because she is rumoured to have played with loaded dice).

Like many modern Christmases, the Tudor seasonal celebrations were not terribly religious in focus. Even in the court, the secular festivities of Christmas sports, merriment and feasting were far more popular than any pious observances. The most boisterous and rowdy celebrations took place on Twelfth Night (the evening of 5 January). By the turn of the 17th century, this lack of piety around Christmas time was beginning to enrage the more austere elements of the Church, and trouble was brewing . . .

The Puritans who stole Christmas

In an extraordinary act of miserly mean-spiritedness, the 17th-century Puritan parliament under Oliver Cromwell pulled the plug on all festive frivolity. To the Puritans, Christmas was just an excuse for chaos, extravagance, immorality and debauchery, and worse than all that, they linked it with Catholicism (the word Christmas comes from Christ's Mass). And that simply wouldn't do.

In the 1640s the Long Parliament began to clamp down on what they dubbed 'Satan's working day', demanding that it be referred to as 'Christ-tide' and observed only as a day of fasting and prayer. In 1644, an Act of Parliament banned all forms of celebration during the 12 days of Christmas and in 1647 an Ordinance made it abundantly clear that the feasts of Christmas, Easter and Whitsun were illegal.

Things went from bad to worse. During the 1650s the army was deployed on the streets of London to forcibly confiscate any illicit Christmas goodies and further laws banned Christmas carols and nativity scenes, and forced shops and businesses to stay open on 25 December. Any heathens found attending a Christmas church service could be fined, or even put in the stocks. Christmas was well and truly cancelled.

Some were so outraged by the ban that they took to the streets, and there were violent confrontations in many towns in England. But most people simply went underground. For 18 long years, Christmas celebrations were confined to the home.

After the monarchy and Christmas were restored in 1660, people did not resume the seasonal festivities with the same gusto as they had before. For many, Christmas as a time of rejoicing had almost been forgotten in those 18 years, and there was no popular movement to restore it. Some argue that Christmas celebrations could even have died out had it not been for the work of one man.

The man credited with saving Christmas is William Winstanley, the son of an Essex farmer. During the Christmas ban he had held clandestine carol services in his family home, inviting fellow supporters to join him. But it was after the restoration that he really made a difference. Winstanley made it his mission to restore Christmas to its former glory, writing extensively about the joys of the season and lobbying the aristocracy to pave the way by opening their houses for feasting, dancing and carolling. For 38 years until his death he persistently kept up a stream of festive propaganda and by the 1680s Christmas had taken root again.

Despite his work the glory days of the medieval Christmas feasts were well and truly over and Christmas became a quieter, more sombre occasion for rich and poor alike. Although Twelfth Night retained its reputation for drunken frivolity, by the 18th century Christmas Day was an ordinary working day for many. It wasn't until the Victorian era that the true spirit of Christmas returned.

Pocket fact ☆

Shakespeare's Twelfth Night *includes a good deal of drunkenness and revelry typical of the rowdy end of Christmas celebrations. The play would have been performed in Elizabethan England as part of the many celebrations that signalled the end of the festive season.*

VICTORIAN CHRISTMAS

Before the 19th century, Christmas celebrations had been largely sponsored by the landowning classes and involved large communal events, complete with unique village customs. But by the time Victoria came to the throne in 1837, Christmas was already morphing into a more private, family-oriented affair. No longer reliant on the goodwill of the wealthy classes, the new urban middle class of doctors, merchants, bankers and shopkeepers headed up the revival of the Christmas spirit.

The invention of the railway and improved transport links encouraged families to get together at Christmas time and also helped to create national, rather than local, festive traditions.

Christmas in the Victorian era was much more a children's festival. Commerce had developed and Britain had become 'a nation of shopkeepers', so presents for the children became integral to the festivities. Old customs like Christmas carols were revived, cards and crackers were invented, and the jolly figure of Father Christmas was embraced with renewed vigour by the new middle classes. Almost all of the elements of Christmas that we know and love today were created or transformed by the Victorians.

Modern-day Christmas traditions from the Victorian era

The Victorian Christmas that we know so well from the writing of Dickens and other prominent Victorian authors was a mixture of old customs, imported traditions and some important innovations:

- **The Christmas tree** – *imported from Germany and embraced by Prince Albert. In fact there had been a Christmas tree at Windsor Castle as far back as the 1790s, but it was Albert's tree that caught the public imagination.*
- **The Christmas cracker** – *invented by sweetshop owner Tom Smith in 1846.*
- **Giving presents** – *previously presents were more closely associated with New Year, but from the 1860s they became a crucial part of the Christmas Day ritual.*
- **The Christmas panto** – *a uniquely English tradition, that had its heyday during the Victorian era. In 1860 HJ Byron wrote his version of Aladdin, which included Dame Widow Twankey.*
- **Christmas cards** – *evolved from calling cards, the first true Christmas card was the idea of one Henry Cole and went on sale in 1843 in Bond Street, London.*
- **Father Christmas** – *we imported the American tradition of Santa Claus, giving renewed vitality to the much older figure of Father Christmas.*

A THOROUGHLY MODERN CHRISTMAS

It's easy to present the festive developments of the 20th and early 21st century in a negative light. Commercialisation, television, shop-bought Christmas puddings and oven-ready turkeys, drink-driving, and a total disregard for the religious origins of the festival, are all bemoaned as indications of society crumbling at the roots, and the loss of a traditional Christmas.

But before you nod in agreement, note that similar negative social commentary can be found at various points right through the centuries of Christmas history. What is astonishing is that throughout a period of such enormous social change, Christmas has survived at all.

The hardy spirit of Christmas endured two world wars, famously inspiring the trench truces and many innovative Christmas lunch recipes during rationing (rabbit followed by carrot cake being the most popular). It has withstood rising divorce rates and the extraordinarily complex family relationships of the 21st century. And it has evolved and adapted to embrace the multi-faith nature of the modern world. It seems that the Christmas spirit is a survivor.

❄ CHRISTMAS AROUND THE WORLD ❄

Each family, each town, and each region have their own distinct ways of celebrating Christmas, and between countries the differences are often very pronounced.

WHEN EXACTLY IS CHRISTMAS?

Different branches of Christianity chose different occasions to celebrate, some in January, March, April and September. Nobody even considered 25 December.

When the Church finally did decide on a date, it was for fairly spurious reasons. Many Christians during the third century believed that the conception of Christ had occurred at the spring equinox, then believed to be 25 March. Count nine months on and you get to the date we know as Christmas today. This suited the Romans nicely, as it was slap bang in the middle of a host of other celebrations.

Further east in Alexandria, the Church settled on 6 January (Epiphany), the date associated with the visit of the Three Wise Men, and to this day Christmas is celebrated on 6 January in many countries, including **Russia.**

Pocket fact ☆

*In **Iceland**, Christmas Eve is family time. Television transmission stops at 5pm, while the family listens to evensong on the radio, opens presents and enjoys Christmas dinner. Transmission begins again at 10pm.*

The confusion over the date, complicated by a switch over from the Julian to the Gregorian calendar, has meant that different countries celebrate Christmas at different times. In **Israel**, the very place where the Son of God was born, the event is commemorated on three different dates each year. Catholic and Protestant celebrations take place on 24 December, Orthodox churches rejoice on 7 January, and the Armenian Christians celebrate Christmas on 19 January.

OTHER SIGNIFICANT DATES

Regardless of the date of Christmas Day, many cultures attach significance to a variety of dates throughout the festive season. For many countries such as **France** and the **Czech Republic**, Christmas Eve is far more important than the day itself. This is when gifts are distributed and the family partakes of the Christmas feast.

Festive dates from around the world

- 6 December — St Nicolas' Day is the date that a variety of Father Christmas-like figures leave gifts for the children in lots of countries including **Hungary, Luxembourg, Austria, Germany** and **Belgium**.

- 13 December — the feast of Santa Lucia in **Scandinavia**. Santa Lucia was a Christian martyr from the fourth century and her day originally marked the winter solstice. In Scandinavian countries young girls celebrate by bringing breakfast in bed to the family, and wearing an evergreen wreath, complete with seven lighted candles, on their heads.

- 23 December — St Thorlakur's Day, named after **Iceland**'s most important native saint. This is the day that the Christmas celebrations begin.

- 30 December — St Basil's Day. In **Greece**, the family enjoys a feast on this significant date, after which the family lifts the table three times for good luck.

- 6 January — Three Kings Day. In **Spain, Argentina** and many other Hispanic countries, this is the day that the magi stop off at the house on their way to Bethlehem, leaving sweets and gifts. This day is celebrated with firework displays and village processions.

- 6 January — Christmas Day in **Russia** (among others). When the first evening star appears in the sky, families begin a feast of 12 courses, one for each of the apostles.

- 6 January — also known as Epiphany. In **Ethiopia**, pilgrims from all over the country arrive at the ancient city of Aksum to bathe in waters that have been blessed by a priest.

- 7 January — Christmas Day for many. **Belarus** has two official holidays for Christmas (25 December and 7 January) because the country has both Catholic and Orthodox believers.

FATHER CHRISTMAS AROUND THE WORLD

We may know the corpulent, bearded gift-giver as Father Christmas or Santa Claus but around the world he answers to many different names including:

- Père Noël in **France**
- Kris Kringle in the **USA**
- Viejito Pascuero in **Chile**
- Kerstman in the **Netherlands**
- Djed Mraz in **Croatia**
- Baba Chaghaloo in **Afghanistan**

While there are many similarities between our Father Christmas and his cosmopolitan counterparts, there are also some extraordinary differences.

Firstly, his image is far from universal. While Hollywood has sought to reinforce the jolly, hirsute figure in a red suit, many cultures have steadfastly retained their own Father Christmas figure. For example, in **Latvia** Father Christmas is a very stern-looking man dressed from head to toe in grey.

Then there's the company he keeps. Our Santa gratefully accepts the help of a herd of reindeer, and many more friendly elves. Yet in other cultures it seems he's not so picky. Black Peter (Zwarte Piet) is a mean character found in **Holland** and **Luxembourg** who either accompanies Santa or visits homes the night before. If the children have been naughty then he is believed to scoop them up, stuff them in his bag and spirit them away.

Another of Santa's more dubious associates is a formidable horned demon known as Krampus. In **Hungary, Croatia, Austria, Slovenia** and **Switzerland**, parents use the image of

Krampus to frighten children into being on their best behaviour. Krampus traditionally carries a bunch of birch sticks, with which he beats particularly naughty children (or at least that's what their parents tell them).

Pocket fact ☆

After the Russian Revolution in 1917, the Bolsheviks abolished figures such as Babushka (see p. 127) and Ded Moroz, a tall figure in red and gold robes who rides in a horse-drawn sleigh. However, Stalin reintroduced the Grandfather Frost figure in 1935, changing the colour of his robes to light blue to disassociate him from the western Father Christmas.

UNUSUAL FESTIVE TRADITIONS

- In **Greece** it is customary for families to suspend a cross over a bowl of water during the 12 days of Christmas. Every day a member of the family must dip the cross and sprinkle the water around the house. This fends off mischievous spirits known as *Killantzaroi* who are believed to come down the chimney at this time of year and cause all kinds of mayhem.

- In Nova Scotia, **Canada**, groups of masked mummers known as *belsnicklers* descend on the neighbourhood demanding treats and making lots of noise. They often quiz children on their behaviour and reward them with sweets if they have been good.

- In Oaxaca, **Mexico**, an annual festival of radishes takes place on 23 December. The *noche de rabanos* commemorates the introduction of the radish by Spanish colonists. Radishes here are enormous, weighing up to 10 lbs. Every year locals hold a contest to see who can carve their radish into the most impressive nativity scene.

- In the **Ukraine** spiders are celebrated as an important part of Christmas folklore. A traditional Ukrainian legend tells of a poor family who were visited by magic spiders at Christmas. The spiders turned all of the webs in the house into silver and gold and the family became rich. As a result spiders are encouraged into the house and a web found on Christmas morning is said to bring good luck.

- In many parts of **Bulgaria**, people fill their house with hay over the Christmas period to remind the family of the stable in which Jesus was born.

- In the **Czech Republic** it is traditional for girls to throw their shoes over their shoulders on Christmas Day. If the toe of the shoe points towards the door, folklore dictates that she will get married that year.

9

TIPS FOR A BETTER CHRISTMAS

❄ PLANNING AHEAD ❄

PLANNING YOUR FINANCES

It is certainly an expensive time of year and even modest house-holds can find that their finances are stretched to the limits. There's all that food and drink to buy, cards to post, new fairy lights and decorations, not to mention the presents for your loved ones. You will find some great tips for a thrifty Christmas on p. 147, but planning your Christmas finances in advance will also help to ease the burden.

> *Pocket fact* ☆
> As a nation, the British spend more than £10 billion on Christmas.

Bank accounts

One good way to do this is to open a Christmas bank account. Many banks and building societies have schemes set up for just this purpose, and the Post Office offers a Christmas Club card that lets you save up to £1,000 on a prepay card that is valid at many high street shops. The idea is that you save a little bit each month, earning interest on your savings, and by Christmas you have accumulated more than enough for a lavish Christmas. The advantage of these schemes is that spending is not enabled until 1 November, preventing you from dipping into your savings early.

Borrowing

Borrowing money at Christmas can be disastrous and you could find yourself paying off the debt for the rest of the year. If you do have to borrow then do so wisely. Apply for a credit card with a 0% introductory rate on spending so that if you can't pay your debts off immediately, you won't be penalised.

Can you make a profit?

If you think you will be able to pay for Christmas in full then look out for cashback credit cards. These cards have a prohibitively high rate of interest so you *must* clear your balance in full. However, they often give you up to 5% cashback for the first three months (up to a maximum spend of around £4,000), so those with their eye on the ball can actually profit from Christmas spending.

Pocket fact ☆

According to a recent survey, while women spend more money on gifts overall at Christmas, men spend more money on socialising and on their partners. Men get the worst deal overall, though, because more money is spent, by both genders, on mothers, daughters and female partners.

SHOPPING PLANNING

Set a budget

Once you have decided how to finance Christmas, it is then a good idea to set an overall budget broken down into its constituent parts. Once you know how much you will spend on food, drink, decorations, and each person's present, then you can start to look for them in advance. Not only does staggering your purchases avoid the stress of a last-minute rush, it also prevents your wallet from suffering one almighty blow.

Think ahead

Of course if you are really organised then you will have bought all your wrapping paper, crackers and Christmas cards in the January sales, when everything is dirt cheap. The chances are you won't have done this, but keep it in mind for next Christmas.

Food and drink

The big Christmas food shop is perhaps one of the most difficult elements to get right. Just look at the evidence: 160,000 tonnes of leftover food is thrown away in the UK every Christmas. The trick is not to buy any Christmas food or drink until you have made a comprehensive list of everything you will need. Supermarkets are experts at tempting you into overspending on special offers and enticing goodies. Going in with a master plan should help to prevent spontaneous supermarket splurges.

PRESENT PLANNING

Buying presents is a skill that comes naturally to some people, but most of us really have to graft. There is nothing worse than desperately roaming the shops, hoping for inspiration. In fact the internet is a far better source of ideas and doesn't involve the lack of parking spaces, heaving crowds, and queues on the high street.

Pocket tip ⛄

Do some internet research while you are making a budget and come up with a list of possible presents for each person.

Mapping your presents out in this way will help prevent you buying 10 gifts for one person and very few for anyone else. If you really don't have a clue then it is far better to ask them for ideas than to buy something that will end up gathering dust on a shelf or in the bin.

The presents that people remember tend to be those that are funny and thoughtful, not necessarily those that are flash and expensive. There are lots of great websites for silly little gifts.

Ideas for stocking fillers

- *A diary*
- *Tickets to the recording of a favourite BBC show (free), available from bbc.co.uk/tickets*
- *Party poppers and streamers*
- *Free samples from the cosmetics counter*
- *Old-fashioned wind-up or wooden toys (try www.daysgonebyshop.co.uk)*
- *Chocolate coins and favourite sweets*
- *A year's subscription to a favourite magazine. Cheap deals are available at www.discountpublications.co.uk*
- *Waterproof iPod pouch (available from www.design-go.com)*
- *Nuts and tangerines*
- *Packs of cards and card games like Uno and Top Trumps*
- *Mini compass and thermometer (available from www.blacks.co.uk)*
- *A Santa hat and musical socks*
- *Useful, reusable Onya bags (available from www.onyabags.co.uk)*

- *A stationery set*
- *Seeds and secateurs for keen gardeners*
- *Origami sticky notes (available from www.suck.uk.com)*
- *Pocket Bibles! (available from www.crimsonpublishing.co.uk)*

SECRET SANTA

Secret Santa is a relatively modern Christmas tradition popular with offices, schools and large families. It's a great way to minimise the cost of Christmas as each person buys a gift for just one other person, chosen by selecting a name from a hat. They then have an agreed limit (usually £5, £10 or £20) with which to buy a gift. The presents are often given anonymously, allowing great scope for amusing, creative and slightly cheeky gift-giving.

Not only does Secret Santa keep costs down, but it also brings everyone together and adds an element of fun to the proceedings, although in the office environment the anonymity of the scheme has sometimes given rise to offensive and inappropriate gifts. Try to avoid giving deodorant, a toothbrush or any amusingly shaped novelty items if you still want a job/friends/family in the New Year.

CHRISTMAS PLANNING CHECKLIST

The earlier you start planning Christmas, the less stressful it will be. The super-organised begin thinking about Christmas in September, or even start to buy presents in the summer sales, but for the rest of us mere mortals, this 10-week plan should help:

Mid-October

- Get the diary out and mark all the parties, concerts and gatherings for the coming 10 weeks. This allows you to schedule when to cook, clean, shop and decorate in plenty of time.

- Plan your Christmas entertaining. If you're having a Christmas party, start thinking now about what you will need.

- Work out your Christmas budget and make a gift list. If you have planned your gifts early, you can stagger your buying and keep ahead of the game.

Early November

- Plan your Christmas meals and make a list of all the food and drink you will need. Order your Christmas meat and also place orders for drinks and food. If you're planning on a booze cruise, go as early as possible to beat the rush.

- Send out your invitations for any festive gatherings you have planned. People get booked up quickly over the festive period.

- If you are making any edible presents such as jams or chutneys, now is the time to do it.

- Make any online present orders to avoid inflated Christmas postal prices and leave yourself plenty of time for them to arrive.

- If you are planning on hosting a large number of guests, check you have enough cutlery, china, glasses, serving dishes, roasting trays and so on. This will give you plenty of time to buy anything you are short of.

Mid-November

- Buy your wrapping paper, crackers and Christmas cards, if you didn't get them in the January sales.

- Get the box of decorations down from the loft, sort out the inevitable tangled mess and test your fairy lights. If you need to make or buy any new decorations there is still plenty of time.

- Defrost and clean out the freezer so that there's plenty of room for all the Christmas supplies.

- Purchase the remainder of your gifts throughout November, and remember to wrap as you buy to save time later.

- If you are going to need a babysitter over the festive period, now is the time to book one, as they will get booked up fast.

- If you are making Christmas pudding and cake, you need to start now.

Early December

- Time for a thorough clean of the house, including any hard-to-reach places like ceilings, corners, under the sofas and tables. A comprehensive clean and purge now will mean you can easily keep everything tidy throughout December.

- Start making dishes for the freezer such as meals for the family and dishes for entertaining. All sauces can be made in advance and frozen, and so can mince pies, desserts and vegetable dishes.

- Write your Christmas cards and post them.

- Start thinking about the big Christmas food shop for anything you haven't already bought. If you are planning to order online, you will need to order your delivery slot now.

- Post any Christmas parcels.

Two weeks to go

- Buy your tree, but don't bring it into the house yet.

- Post any last-minute cards and parcels.

- Buy any last-minute presents and stocking fillers.

- Ice and decorate the Christmas cake.

One week to go

- Buy any fresh or perishable foods that you need for the festive period.

- Bring the tree in and get the whole family to help decorate the house.

- Clean out the fridge and make as much space as possible for the vast quantities of festive food that will soon fill it.

- Check how long the turkey will take to defrost and get it out in plenty of time.

Christmas Eve

- Set the stage for Christmas Day by doing any last-minute tidying and cleaning, setting the Christmas table and getting out all the serving dishes you will need.

- Hang out the stockings and leave a glass of sherry and a couple of mince pies for Santa and his reindeer.

❄ TIPS FOR A THRIFTY CHRISTMAS ❄

Commercialism has reigned supreme as king of the festive season for over a century but as we well know, it's not expensive presents and luxury crackers that make a great Christmas. No, the best things in life are free, and the rest can be bought on a budget. Here are some tips to avoid breaking the bank at Christmas:

DECORATING THE HOUSE

- Instead of plastering your house with shiny plastic, why not go green and bring in evergreens from the garden? People have used holly, ivy and mistletoe to decorate their homes during the dark days of winter for thousands of years and it hasn't cost them a thing. These days, of course, holly can be expensive if you don't happen to have it in the garden, but local hedgerows should provide good substitutes, from rose hips to hawthorn berries.

- Buying a new Christmas tree each year can be very expensive, whereas a good artificial tree will last for years and cost as little as £20. If a fake tree is a step too far, then there are evergreen alternatives. A potted box, holly or bay can live in your garden for most of the year and be brought inside over the festive period to be decorated.

- Avoid false economies with the fairy lights. Cheap lights tend to pack up entirely if just one bulb goes, so it's best to invest in a heavy-duty set that will last for years.

- Make your own decorations. If you have restless children, or even if you don't, there's a lot more fun to be had from making your own paper chains out of colourful magazines and last year's cards. And you will gain brownie points for being green. There are lots of good ideas in the Make Your Own chapter (p. 81).

- Instead of throwing money away on wrapping paper, use up leftover bits of wallpaper, or use cheaper brown parcel paper or tissue paper.

STOCKING UP ON FOOD AND DRINK

- If you have lots of guests, or you're planning a big Christmas party, it can work out much cheaper to set off on a booze cruise to France. Off-licence chains such as Majestic and Oddbins often have free ferry or cashback deals that can lead to real savings. Depending on the exchange rate, it can also be worth popping into the hypermarket for savings on Christmas foodstuffs.

- Some of the big UK supermarkets, such as Tesco and Sainsbury's offer Christmas savings clubs, where points accumulated during the year are 'locked in' until your big Christmas shop. Members of these clubs also receive special offer coupons.

- Don't snub the discount supermarkets like Aldi and Lidl, where luxury items are sometimes incredibly cheap. To shop around for the best deals, try www.mysupermarket.co.uk.

How to get yourself into the Christmas spirit

- *Invite friends round for a few carols around the piano, complete with mulled wine and festive nibbles.*
- *Make your own mince pies, preferably while listening to the carols from King's College, Cambridge.*
- *Visit your local church for a carol service or Christingle service.*
- *Go ice-skating at one of the outdoor ice rinks that appear in the lead-up to Christmas.*
- *Watch one of the great Christmas films, like* Elf, It's a Wonderful Life, *or* White Christmas.
- *Book tickets for your local pantomime. The jokes will be bad, the celebrities Z-list, and the story implausible, but it will definitely get you in the mood.*
- *Gather holly, ivy and mistletoe and make your own Christmas wreaths, see p. 81.*
- *Go to one of the many Christmas markets or frost fairs that take place across the country in December.*
- *Indulge in the ancient tradition of wassailing, see p. 5.*
- *Decorate the tree with fairy lights and gather the family together for a switching-on ceremony.*

SENDING CHRISTMAS CARDS

- Rather than spending a fortune on cards and postage, send your season's greetings electronically via an e-card. Not only is it free, but it's also more environmentally friendly than the real thing.

- Alternatively, you can make your own cards, either by printing out photos, or getting the children to do simple potato prints onto coloured card.

BUYING PRESENTS

- Agree a limit with friends and family for each gift. Actually trying to find good presents for, say, under £5, requires a lot more creativity and the results are often more memorable.

- Making your own presents may sound like a hassle, but it will save you money and add the personal touch to your gifts. You will find ideas for jams and chutneys on p. 88. Other good ideas include planting cuttings from your favourite plants into attractively decorated pots and printing out photos and making albums or calendars.

- Take advantage of the offers on the high street. Shops like WH Smith and Boots often offer three-for-two promotions at Christmas, which are really useful for stocking fillers.

- A good trick is to save up your loyalty card points, from chains such as Boots, Tesco and Sainsbury's, throughout the year and cash them in when you really need them – at Christmas.

- Do as much of your shopping online as you can. The internet has made it far easier to compare prices and websites are often cheaper than you will find on the high street. Remember to allow for postage and delivery charges. Most people fall into the trap of only visiting a few familiar websites, but you can often get better deals by shopping around with price comparison sites such as www.kelkoo.co.uk and www.pricerunner.co.uk. For books and CDs, useful comparison websites are www.find-book.co.uk and www.find-cd.co.uk. For discounted toys try www.thetoyshop.com.

- Keep your eyes peeled for website discount codes. These generally appear online but they are also to be found in newspaper adverts and flyers. These codes often entitle shoppers to a discount or free delivery and there are some great offers. The website www.myvouchercodes.com will help you to stretch your Christmas budget.

❄ TIPS FOR A GREENER CHRISTMAS ❄

'Tis the season of excessive consumption. It is estimated that UK households generate a whopping three million tonnes of extra rubbish over the 12 days of Christmas, most of which ends up in landfill sites, not to mention the extra electricity and other resources wasted at this time of year. So, this year, give the planet a present and follow these simple tips to save money, reduce your Christmas carbon footprint and enjoy more sustainable festivities.

FAIRY LIGHTS

Leaving your fairy lights on for 10 hours a day over the 12 days of Christmas produces enough carbon dioxide to inflate 12 balloons. One way to reduce your carbon footprint is to simply turn them off when they are not needed. It's simple but effective. You can also switch to LED lights, or choose fairy lights that are solar-powered or use rechargeable batteries. You could also offset the extra usage by changing the other lights in the house to energy-saving bulbs.

WRAPPING PAPER

According to Defra (the Department for Environment, Food and Rural Affairs), we throw away enough wrapping paper each year to wrap up the entire island of Guernsey, and if we could recycle just half of the 8,000 tonnes we throw away, we would save 25,000 trees. Unfortunately, not all local authorities will accept wrapping paper as it's often laminated, dyed or covered in sticky tape, making it difficult to recycle. Buying recycled paper in the first instance will certainly help, or try wrapping your presents in brown paper, newspaper, magazine images, or recycled foil. Using string, raffia or ribbon rather than sticky tape will also help.

CHRISTMAS TREES

Real trees are the more eco-friendly choice, but each year we buy around six million Christmas trees as a nation – enough to stretch end to end from London to the North Pole, according to Defra. Yet we recycle less than 10% of these trees, and less than 5% are planted to be reused the next year. To reduce your Christmas carbon footprint, make sure you buy your tree from a sustainable source. More than 400 Christmas tree growers across the UK are registered with the British Christmas Tree Growers' Association and follow strict guidelines. You should also choose a tree with roots so that it can be replanted. If you don't have space to replant, then take your tree to the local recycling depot where it can be turned into wood chippings or compost.

DECORATIONS

Cheap artificial decorations do not biodegrade and often travel thousands of miles from the Far East before reaching your home. It is far greener to decorate your house and tree with organic, recycled and scrap materials such as holly, ivy and even popcorn (see p. 83).

CHRISTMAS FOOD

During the Christmas period, we throw away 80% more food waste than at any other time. Make sure you use up your leftovers – try the turkey curry recipe on p. 158 – and look for other ideas on www.lovefoodhatewaste.com. Recycle any food that you can't use up. Many local authorities collect kitchen waste these days and anything else can be added to your compost heap.

CANDLES

The most eco-friendly candles are biodegradable and smoke free. Try soy, beeswax or natural vegetable-based candles. Paraffin candles are not good for the environment as they are made from petroleum residues.

CHRISTMAS CARDS

Buying recycled or charity cards, or cutting up last year's and making your own, will certainly help. Sending e-cards is also a very effective way of cutting your carbon footprint.

Pocket fact ☆

Every person in the UK sends an average of 17 cards each year.

The Woodland Trust recycles around 93 million of the cards we send every year, allowing it to plant 22,000 trees. The charity sets up collection boxes in participating retailers across the UK.

PRESENTS

Every Christmas around 4,000 tonnes of gifts arrive in the UK from China, before appearing under the Christmas tree. When you are buying presents, try to buy locally, supporting small suppliers and the local community. Try also to buy presents that are durable and don't rely on batteries, and preferably that come with minimal packaging. A quarter of the product price of perfume sets, for example, goes towards the packaging. Gift experiences can be particularly green, as can charity sponsorship gifts. But however green you are, you can't predict the unwanted presents you will receive. Try to avoid throwing gifts away and instead subtly re-gift them at an opportune moment or give them to local charities and hospitals.

BOXING DAY

❊ THE ORIGINS OF BOXING DAY ❊

The most commonly accepted theory as to why we refer to it as Boxing Day dates from the charity of feudal times. The serfs, who often had to work on Christmas Day, would be allowed to take St Stephen's Day as a holiday and as a thank-you for the year's work they would receive boxes filled with practical goods such as cloth, grain and tools from their lord.

Pocket fact ☆

Celebrated in the UK, Australia, New Zealand, Canada and some other Commonwealth countries, 26 December has been a UK bank holiday since 1871.

In later years, the master of the house would present a box of tips to his servants when they arrived at work the day after Christmas. So the practice continued, and in a way, those who leave annual tips to their binmen and postmen are carrying the tradition on to this day.

However, the origins of Boxing Day are somewhat murky and there's a whole host of equally plausible explanations, including:

- 26 December was the day that the alms boxes were opened in church and the money that had been collected over the course of the year was doled out to the parish needy.

- According to the tradition of the 'cutty wren' (see below), the king of the birds was captured on the day after Christmas and put in a box before being paraded around the village. Each household would ask the wren for a successful year and a good harvest.

- In artisan shops, a clay box was placed on the counter for customers to fill with seasonal goodwill, and for employers to give anonymous bonuses. On the day after Christmas, the box was smashed and the contents distributed among the workers.

❄ WHAT TO DO ON BOXING DAY ❄

After all the excitement and build-up, Boxing Day can be a huge letdown. With its charitable roots now a dim memory, it has become a holiday with presents that have already been opened and a dinner that has been eaten. Apparently, one in 20 of us spend it battling with each other at the sales, while the rest, perhaps suffering from the modern Christmas ailment of Wii-knee, slump in front of the television wondering lethargically what to do next. Well, here are some suggestions for a Boxing Day with a difference.

- **Throw yourself into the North Sea.** The Boxing Day dip is a modern British tradition that the brave and the insane have embraced with equal vigour. The oldest and most bizarre takes place at Seaburn Beach near Sunderland and attracts over 1,000 lunatics in fancy dress each year. Why not join them?

- **Hunt the cutty wren.** An old folk custom that survives in odd pockets of rural Britain and Ireland takes place on St Stephen's Day. It is shrouded in legend and folklore but essentially involves hunting down a wren and sacrificing it, accompanied by the singing of the traditional folk song, *The Cutty Wren*. Why? Well, the wren is the king of the birds, and the ancient Greeks believed its annual sacrifice brought good luck and signified the beginning of a new year. Another legend states that the hiding place of Christian martyr St Stephen was betrayed by a chattering wren, which attracted his enemies. And the pagan druids believed the feathers of the wren could protect against witchcraft. All good reasons to finish it off and parade it round the village on a stick. Modern day interpretations of this ritual use a fake wren of course.

- **Race ducks.** If you are looking for a more gentle ornithological pursuit, then head for the annual Boxing Day Duck Race in Kenilworth, Warwickshire. The ducks in question are in fact of the rubber variety and are released into Finham Brook, while spectators bet £1 on their favourite to win.

- **Drink while you sprint.** If you've ever wondered what the fun element of a 'fun run' is, then the Haslemere Boxing Day Fun Run in Surrey has come up with an answer. Participants must down a pint of winter ale two miles into the 3.5-mile run. Actually this is much more fun for the spectators, who are recommended to have a bucket at the ready and wear full-body waterproofs.

Pocket fact ☆

If you can afford to travel to the Bahamas, you'll find none of the lethargy of the British Boxing Day. Their annual Boxing Day festival, called Junkanoo, involves a street parade with traditional rhythmic dancers and elaborate costumes.

❊ BOXING DAY FOOD ❊

Some people rate Boxing Day food as their favourite part of the whole festive gastronomic experience. Cold turkey and ham, served with jacket potatoes or mash, coleslaw, salad and various chutneys and pickles, offer the traditional healthy feast, enough to attract even those who are still groaning from the previous day's over-indulgence.

But if you fancy a change this Christmas, and your fridge is bulging with leftovers, why not try this simple curry?

Pocket Recipe: Easy turkey and parsnip curry (serves 4)

Healthy and full of flavour, this post-Christmas curry is easy to make and because it's all cooked in one pan, there's very little washing up.

500g cooked turkey
Leftover vegetables
2 tbsp vegetable oil
2 onions
500g parsnips
5 tbsp Madras curry paste
400g can chopped tomatoes
150g pot low-fat natural yoghurt
Basmati rice

1. Chop the onions in half (through the root) and slice thinly. Add to oil that has been lightly heated in a saucepan and fry for 10 minutes on a low heat until they are softened and coloured. Chop up the parsnips and add to the pan. Stir well.

2. Stir in the curry paste and add the tomatoes with a pinch of salt and stir well. Add 1½ canfulls of water and bring to the boil. Reduce the heat, cover the pan and simmer for around 20 minutes, until the parsnips are tender. Add in any left over vegetables from Christmas Day lunch. Potatoes, carrots, squash and even sprouts will all taste great.

3. Chop your leftover turkey into chunks and stir into the pan. Cover the pan and simmer for a further 5 minutes, making sure the turkey is heated through.

4. Remove from the heat and lightly stir in the yoghurt. Serve with basmati rice.

Boxing Day events in recent history

- **2006** – *The Iraqi Appeals Court turns down Saddam Hussein's appeal against the death sentence.*
- **2004** – *At least 283,000 people were killed and many more lost their homes as a tsunami, triggered by a 9.0 magnitude earthquake under the Indian Ocean, hit southern Asia.*
- **1991** – *The USSR's parliament formally voted the country out of existence.*
- **1990** – *Iran's spiritual leader, Ayatollah Ali Khamenei, upheld the fatwa on writer Salman Rushdie for alleged blasphemy.*
- **1956** – *Fidel Castro attempted a secret landing to overthrow the Batista regime in Cuba. All but 11 of his supporters were killed.*
- **1941** – *Less than three weeks after America's entrance into the Second World War, Winston Churchill becomes the first British Prime Minister to address the US Congress.*
- **1908** – *A real Boxing Day first, Jack Johnson became the first black boxer to win the world heavyweight title.*

NEW YEAR CELEBRATIONS

❄ AULD LANG SYNE ❄

The most famous song in the world to which no-one knows the words, *Auld Lang Syne* was first published in 1796 by the Scottish poet, Robert Burns, in *Scots Musical Museum*. Although Burns made some additions of his own to the lyrics, the song itself is a traditional verse from Ayrshire and means 'times gone by'.

The tune didn't become a bona fide New Year's tradition, however, until after 1929 when it was popularised by Guy Lombardo and his Royal Canadians, at a party in the Roosevelt Grill in New York. This performance, featuring *Auld Lang Syne* at the stroke of midnight was broadcast live across North America and became an annual tradition after Lombardo moved his band to the Waldorf Hotel in the mid-1930s.

Auld Lang Syne
(Robert Burns 1759–1796)

> Should auld acquaintance be forgot,
> And never brought to mind?
> Should auld acquaintance be forgot,
> And auld lang syne?

CHORUS
For auld lang syne, my dear,
For auld lang syne,
We'll tak a cup o' kindness yet,
For auld lang syne.

And surely ye'll be your pint-stowp,
And surely I'll be mine!
And we'll tak a cup o' kindness yet,
For auld lang syne.

We twa hae run about the braes,
And pu'd the gowans fine;
But we've wandered mony a weary fit
Sin' auld lang syne.

We twa hae paidled i' the burn,
Frae morning sun till dine;
But seas between us braid hae roared
Sin' auld lang syne.

And there's a hand, my trusty fiere,
And gie's a hand o' thine!
And we'll tak a right guid-willie waught
For auld lang syne.

❄ FIRST FOOTING ❄

The tradition of first footing is particular to Celtic regions of the UK. Variations of the custom can be found in Worcestershire, Wales and Yorkshire, though it remains strongest in Scotland at Hogmanay. The 'first foot' is the first person to come through a household's front door after midnight on New Year's Eve. The first foot also affects the luck and prosperity of the household for the coming year. Tall, dark, handsome, male strangers are generally considered perfect 'first foots' (or is that first dates?) – in previous times, women first footers were viewed with a dread, second only to red- or fair-haired males (this is probably a hangover from the early Viking raids).

A good first foot should also come bearing gifts; traditionally, coal for warmth, salt for wealth, a black bun for food, and a bottle – usually whisky.

❄ PARTY IDEAS ❄

It's not New Year's Eve without a party. Here are a couple of ideas to put the pop back in your seasonal popularity.

A NEW YEAR GAME

I Resolve . . .

A variation on a modern classic, this game requires sticky notes and pens.

- Divide the guests into pairs.

- Each couple writes a secret New Year's resolution for their partner on a sticky note and places it on their partner's forehead. Individuals must not know their own resolution.

- Going round a circle, every player tries to guess their resolution by asking questions with yes/no answers.

- Players continue to ask questions until they receive a 'No' answer. Then questioning passes to the next player.

- The first player to correctly guess their resolution wins.

Pocket fact ☆

For holiday romance, New Year's Eve beats even Valentine's Day for marriage proposals.

NEW YEAR DRINK

Nothing says New Year's Eve like Champagne, and Champagne cocktails can really get a party started. Especially one called . . .

Pocket Recipe: Happy New Year Cocktail

7 ml brandy
21 ml ruby port
21 ml orange juice
7 ml Champagne

Shake together the brandy, port and orange juice over ice. Strain into a Champagne flute and top up with bubbly. Happy New Year.

❄ NEW YEAR RESOLUTIONS ❄

This dates back to the ancient Babylonian custom of returning things that had been borrowed over the previous year, and so mankind has been consistently failing to keep New Year resolutions for about 4,000 years. The custom was then adapted by the Romans around the second century when the god Janus officially took over January. With his two faces, Janus was believed to look backwards and forwards through time simultaneously and it became customary to settle old scores and disputes before January began.

Pocket fact ☆

Losing weight is reckoned to be the world's most frequently made (and broken) New Year's Resolution.

❊ NEW YEAR CELEBRATIONS AROUND THE WORLD ❊

CHINA – YUAN TAN (SPRING FESTIVAL)

Spring Festival or Lunar Festival is the biggest Chinese holiday for the majority of mainland Chinese and runs from the first to 15th day of the new lunar year, falling between mid-January and mid-February. Yuan Tan is a time when housekeeping, both physical and metaphorical, is done. Houses are cleaned from top to bottom and old debts are paid so that all bad luck from the previous year can be swept away. New Year's Eve night is a time for family and the spirits of ancestors are said to join the current generation around the dinner table. Fireworks are released everywhere at midnight.

INDIA – DIAL

The Festival of Lights is almost universally celebrated across India with the lighting of candles or divas. Falling on the night of the new moon, between mid-October to mid-November, this national holiday unites regional and religious differences. Originally a harvest festival, the celebrations are held over five days with dazzling displays of fireworks, flowers, lights and dance.

JAPAN – SHOGATSU

Probably the most important Japanese holiday, Shogatsu is celebrated from 1–3 January and is a time to put the previous year behind you. New Year's Eve is celebrated with bonenkai or 'year forgetting party' and money is often handed out to children in colourful envelopes called *otoshidama-bukuro*. It is also considered important to watch the first sunrise of the New Year.

Pocket fact ☆

The 2009 New Year fireworks display over the River Thames in London cost an estimated £1.6m for about 15 minutes.

IRAN – NOWRUZ

The Iranian New Year usually occurs around 21 March and falls on the day containing the moment of the vernal (spring) equinox and the official start to spring.

Associated with the Zoroastrian tradition, Nowruz is a time for house-cleaning and preparing for the new, with new clothes and brief, ritual visits to the homes of close family and friends.

SCOTLAND – HOGMANAY

Probably the UK's most vibrant New Year celebrations take place across Scotland every 31 December in a barrage of pagan fire and pipe bands. While the tradition of first footing (see p. 161) persists throughout Scotland, as does the swinging of home-made fire balls in Stonehaven, the old traditions are gradually being supplemented by the new, such as Loony Dook, in which foolhardy celebrators clad in fancy dress take a New Year's morning dip in the frosty waters of Edinburgh's River Forth.

INDEX

THE DOG LOVER'S POCKET BIBLE

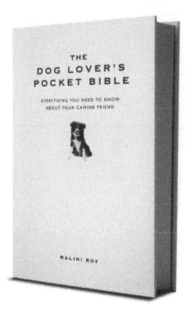

Dogs are wonderful animals and dedicated pets, having enjoyed the title of 'man's best friend' for centuries; they provide companionship and hours of joy to adults and children across the world. Immerse yourself in fascinating trivia and handy tips and tricks for your faithful companion.

978-1-90708-703-5

Available now

£9.99

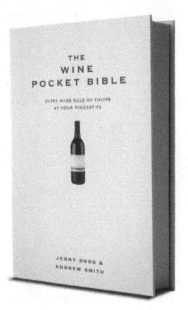

THE COOK'S
POCKET BIBLE

Even the most experienced cook has questions. After all, no one can remember everything they need to when they're in the kitchen – from how long a 16lb turkey will take to roast, to which bits of a dragon fruit you can eat. *The Cook's Pocket Bible* puts the answers to all those on-the-spot questions right at your floured fingertips.

THE GARDENER'S
POCKET BIBLE

Do you know every gardening technique and rule of thumb off pat? How deep should you plant these bulbs? Are you supposed to prune the roses now, or in February? Is it OK to plant out these seedlings now? *The Gardener's Pocket Bible* gives you on-the-spot answers to all your gardening questions and more.